I0185680

PRAISE FOR:

BUT... GOD GAVE ME A PENCIL

You should read *But...God Gave Me a Pencil* if you want to be inspired by the extraordinary journey of Dr. Rhonda Richmond. Born into a world with minimal support, she graduated from high school unable to read. Despite this, she now holds two master's degrees and a doctorate and leads a national organization that impacts thousands of youth across the country. Her story is a testament to resilience and determination.

Even more important, if you have a child or influence the life of a child struggling to learn, this book is a must-read. It will guide and inspire you. It will give you a step-by-step process to help your child learn and succeed in school.

Rhonda's path to success was fraught with challenges, yet she persevered and, in turn, found ways to help her children thrive. Though her journey was arduous, she was supported by those who guided her along the way. You might be that guiding light for someone else. If you aspire to make a significant impact, read this book.

—**Debbi Speck**, president emeritus, *Elevate USA*

***

Loved it!

Dr. Rhonda's unwavering determination and tenacity serve as a source of empowerment and motivation for readers looking to achieve their own goals. It highlights her story as a testament to the boundless power of perseverance and the remarkable feats that can be accomplished when individuals refuse to be hindered by their circumstances. Dr. Rhonda's narrative is sure to resonate deeply with those seeking inspiration and a renewed sense of purpose in their own journeys.

—**Crystal Auguste,** executive director, *Elevate Savannah*

***

Dr. Richmond, you are persistent passion personified, and *But...God Gave Me a Pencil* exemplifies the incredible gifts you bring to this world. From being abandoned and navigating the foster care system, to becoming a leader in literacy and special education, your journey is profoundly inspiring. And your resilience in overcoming illiteracy and developing innovative teaching methods is nothing short of groundbreaking. This memoir, and your relentless advocacy through your ongoing work, continue to impact the lives of the voiceless many who struggle with learning difficulties and those who wish to help but are uncertain how. Truly grateful for the friendship and mentorship – as you help me to see people and the world through new eyes.

—**Dan Streeter,** CEO, *Mission Fuel*

***

BUT…God Gave Me a Pencil is a profound and moving memoir that traces Dr. Rhonda Richmond's incredible journey from abandonment and illiteracy to becoming a champion of hope and change for neurodiversity and education. Dr. Richmond's candid storytelling reveals her struggles before and after her diagnosis of autism and learning disabilities, offering an authentic perspective on overcoming adversity. This book is a must-read for anyone seeking to understand the complexities of learning disabilities and the extraordinary potential within every individual to triumph against the odds and make a lasting impact on the world. Dr. Richmond's story is a testament to the power of resilience, parental advocacy, and the belief that every child deserves a chance to succeed.

—**Dina Caraballo,** former special education teacher; software engineer

***

Blessed with a natural talent for storytelling and teaching, Dr. Rhonda Richmond drew me into her deeply personal narrative of struggle and triumph. As a layperson, I found her memoir an enlightening exploration of the systemic barriers faced by individuals with disabilities. Dr. Rhonda challenged my preconceived notions and provided comprehensive answers to all my questions. This book is an essential resource and a lifeline for anyone seeking to understand and support the neurodiverse community.

—**Jonas Cayo,** president/CEO, *Elevate Orlando*

***

In *BUT...God Gave Me a Pencil,* Dr. Rhonda Richmond shares a deeply moving and inspirational journey that highlights the power of resilience and the transformative impact of embracing one's unique abilities. Dr. Richmond's story is a testament to the power of resilience.

As someone who has had the privilege of knowing Dr. Richmond personally, I can attest to her unwavering determination and incredible spirit. Not only is she a remarkable author and educator, but she is also a cherished friend and mentor who continues to inspire me every day.

Dr. Richmond's candid reflections on overcoming immense personal and educational obstacles offer invaluable insights into the lived experience of neurodiversity. Despite graduating high school functionally illiterate, her relentless pursuit of literacy and innovative approach to teaching her own children laid the foundation for her later success as an educator and leader. Now, as the chief program officer of a national mentorship organization, Dr. Richmond channels her experiences into training and inspiring others.

BUT...God Gave Me a Pencil is more than just a memoir; it is a beacon of hope and a call to action for educators, parents, and anyone facing their own battles with adversity. Dr. Richmond's story is a shining example of how embracing neurodiversity can lead to profound personal and societal change. This book is a must-read for anyone seeking to understand the transformative power of resilience and the boundless potential of the human spirit.

—**Gilda Gomez**, mother, wife

***

Dr. Richmond's book offers an incredibly valuable and vulnerable perspective. Her narrative provides a window into the challenges and beauty of navigating a world not fully understood by others. As a parent of a neurodivergent child and a professional with a long career working with young people, I found this book deeply enlightening and thought-provoking. It feels like a must-read for anyone working with youth, parents or guardians of children with or without neurodiverse diagnoses, individuals who have felt othered due to their conditions, and anyone curious about autism and learning disabilities.

—**Susan Duncombe,** MSW, LCSW, founder and principal consultant of *Wholehearted Consulting, LLC.*

BUT...
GOD GAVE ME
A
PENCIL

DR. RHONDA RICHMOND

Published by KHARIS PUBLISHING, an imprint of
KHARIS MEDIA LLC.

Copyright © 2024 Dr. Rhonda Richmond
ISBN-13: 978-1-63746-262-1
ISBN-10: 1-63746-262-X
Library of Congress Control Number: 2024943904
All rights reserved. This book or parts thereof may not be
reproduced in any form, stored in a retrieval system, or
transmitted in any form by any means - electronic, mechanical,
photocopy, recording, or otherwise - without prior written
permission of the publisher, except as provided by United States
of America copyright law.

All KHARIS PUBLISHING products are available at special
quantity discounts for bulk purchase for sales promotions,
premiums, fund-raising, and educational needs. For details,
contact:
Kharis Media LLC
Tel: 1-630-909-3405
support@kharispublishing.com
www.kharispublishing.com

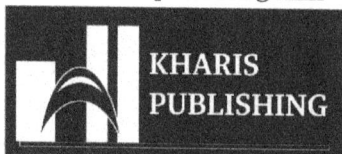

This book is dedicated to my amazing husband, Robbi. Thank you for a beautiful life. I would never have imagined that a poem sent by email would result in life-long love. I don't know how to be in space without you. You are indeed my other half. I praise God for you because you are the gift that makes my soul shine.

Acknowledgments

When I look back at my life, I know – without a doubt – that I did not get to where I am alone. There are numerous people who supported and coached me along the way. Every person I met was meant to be part of my journey in some way; they were present to teach me lessons about love, trust, responsibility, respect, resilience, having a teachable spirit, and, most of all, they made way for me to be able to support others. On this single page, I can't list everyone who has supported me, but they have included family, framily (friends who became family), friends, mentees, mentors, antagonists, and cheerleaders alike.

TABLE OF CONTENTS

PREFACE

*"We know that affliction produces endurance, endurance
produces proven character, and proven character produces hope.
This hope will not disappoint us, because God's love has been
poured out in our hearts through the Holy Spirit
who was given to us."*
Romans 5:1-5

Several times, people I meet ask me to describe what
it is like to think the way I do. Those who ask tend
to qualify their statements with phrases like, "This is
not normal," or, "This is not typical of how people
think." I must admit that it's a curious endeavor to
encapsulate what it's like to live disabled—my distinct
perspective that veers from the elusive "norm." It's not
that I don't have the vocabulary to describe how I feel,
but how does one determine the difference in the
flavors of two fruits, having never experienced one of
the flavors? I've never known "normal"; I've only been
measured by it. So when some people compare me to
"normal", I feel exposed as a fraud. Since this book is
my attempt to provide some detail about how I
experience life, I will start by explaining more about my
diagnosis.

Autism Spectrum Disorder (ASD) is a neurodevelopmental condition affecting cognitive abilities, social interactions, communication, and behavior. Before 2013, autism was recognized as a developmental disorder that included pervasive developmental disorder-not otherwise specified (PDD-NOS); Asperger's syndrome (AD); at the mild end of the spectrum, childhood disintegrative disorder (CDD), which was characterized by severe developmental reversals and regressions, and Rett syndrome, affecting movement and communication, primarily in girls.

Initially, I was diagnosed with Asperger's syndrome in 2012, according to the criteria of the Diagnostic and Statistical Manual of Mental Disorders -Text Revision (*DSM IV-TR*©, American Psychiatric Association (APA), 1994). In 2013, the revised *DSM-V* ©replaced that earlier edition and some of the diagnostic criteria across disorders changed. Those changes are important, especially as they refer to Autism Spectrum Disorders (ASDs), my story, and to explaining the unique experiences of people diagnosed with autism.

Asperger's Syndrome, as defined by the *DSM-IV-TR*©, was classified as part of the ASD that was characterized by repetitive patterns of behavior, preoccupation with restricted interests, and difficulties with social interactions, without intellectual impairment or significant problems with verbal communication. Five main symptoms were apparent during a diagnosis that included obsessing over a single interest, craving routine, missing social cues, limited to no eye contact and inability to understand social thinking.

At the time of my diagnosis, I was informed that an individual with Asperger's might possess mild language delays, have average to above-average intelligence, but struggle with social interactions and interpersonal communication. In contrast, someone with another autism classification might have a cognitive delay impacting their language expression and more visible stimming behaviors (repeated movements or utterances), and they would typically be diagnosed early in life. During this time, I did a great deal of internet research, and I admit I was nervous about the diagnosis because so much of what I found described the negative impact of autism. Autistic people in research studies were portrayed as helpless victims to be cured. Following the change in 2013, I moved from an Asperger's diagnosis to the inclusive diagnosis of Autism Spectrum Disorder (ASD).

I was not accurately diagnosed during my childhood for two reasons. The first reason is that girls are often misrepresented, misdiagnosed, or diagnosed later in life because we tend to mask our symptoms socially by mimicking other people. This explains my "Punky Brewster" phase, when I began wearing multiple layers of socks because I watched too much television.

What some people do not understand is that every person with autism manifests the disorder differently. One person might have a learning disability, another might have more impaired social abilities, and another could be impacted in a variety of other ways. A statement I heard most accurately reflects this: "Once you have met one person with autism, you've met one person with autism."

My autism is complicated by learning disabilities in reading, writing, and math. What this means is that there are many things I have learned that I cannot share with others because I struggle to get the words out orally or in writing. It made obtaining a doctorate extremely difficult. I love researching, finding gaps in things, and looking for solutions, but my lack of communication skills, blunt communication style, lack of facial expression or eye contact, struggles with spelling and grammar, and a mix-up in a number here and there tend to get in the way.

In these moments when I feel most vulnerable, memories rush forth of classrooms where I raised my hand and where my voice faltered as I dared to confess my lack of comprehension. The response from my instructors was not always one of understanding; it often came in the form of repetition, as if repetition alone held the key to unlocking the mysteries my mind wrestled with.

When I consider explaining how I think, I recall the mounting number of misunderstandings I've had with people because I missed some ambiguous social cues. This pattern has extended in my life well beyond the classroom, reverberating through conversations with family and friends, in which my attempts to inform them about my process have been eclipsed by their frustrations about what I couldn't see in social settings. These significantly complicate working relationships, where I am often dealing with coworkers who have never worked with someone like me and who have never taken the opportunity to truly accept me for the person I am because they cannot see my disabilities.

Not having a physical disability in a world where disabilities are primarily associated with a visible, physical ailment is a challenge. It means that I am often the only voice in the room who is asked to speak on behalf of a much more diverse group of people. It means that I have to always reintroduce people to my limitations without putting up a roadblock to what I am capable of. For instance, when I note that I am not socially aware and that I have social anxiety, people tend to think or act like I am incapable of being in social settings. If I tell people that I just need time and space after an event to calm down, then some people believe that means my anxiety must be too high, therefore, their solution is to remove the obligation altogether.

There are others who presume that if I just act like everyone else, then I would not have any issues. Or, when people know I am autistic, they will try to provide accommodations without talking to me. In their mind, they are "protecting" me; for me, it's just insulting. It's the equivalent of asking for a ladder and getting a one-step, fragile stool to stand on.

Some of my friends and family have told me it's odd that someone who could work hard enough to get a doctorate can struggle with common words or phrases. When I am in a situation where my words refuse to connect to the information I am trying to convey, I find myself physically trying to pull the correct word from my head. I refer to these situations as one of my "combing the refrigerator" moments.

Having a mind that can't find words is like having a room filled with a million filing cabinets with massive amounts of information in each drawer. You stand there, knowing you have used all of the information at some point in your life, but you fail to access the right cabinet to find the correct vocabulary word that expresses the thought your mouth is sharing. Say I am chatting on the phone with someone, and I start to tell that person what I am doing as I'm speaking to them. I might be physically combing my hair while we are talking, but I make the mistake of stating that I am "combing the refrigerator." The person on the phone becomes confused by the statement. I may have missed the error altogether. Typically, that person calls out the error, and then I begin searching for the right word to describe what I was trying to say. I can see the object in my hand but can't get the words out. This happens to me often.

At times, others have made the assumption that my struggles occurred because I was incapable or indifferent to whatever task I was performing at the time. There are also those who presume that my lack of emotional decision-making means I don't care about their feelings - which is not true. Unfortunately, people sometimes express their frustrations with what they call jokes, by excluding me, being rude to me in public, or using words like "retarded, stupid, cold, unfeeling, judgmental, or prideful." Some of these words are coupled with offensive physical movements (such as someone slapping their hand against their chest or their head while using a phrase like "duh") which emphasize harsh social stigmas that I have endured all my life. While not all jokes are ill-intentioned, these assumptions and insults cast a veil over the true nature of my challenges, and the veil is part of the reason that my challenges festered and remained undiagnosed until I turned forty.

My diagnosis took me through many emotions—primarily relief, actually —for finally having answers after years of frustration from being lost in the shadows.

The labels I now bear with my autism are: dyslexia (a neurodevelopmental condition that impacts how someone reads, writes, and spells); dysgraphia (inability to write coherently), and dyscalculia (difficulty with numbers, patterns, and basic mathematical functions). These definitions and details signify milestones in my journey to understand myself better. I am proud of them.

My labels, however, only tell part of my story. My days are punctuated by reminders that guide me through life. In my home, you will often find many stacks of paper with various things written on them. I paint to help me think and remember, so the house has dozens of large paintings. My computer screen is full of windows, and I can't close them because I need to remember to complete a task. I also need multiple spreadsheets to help me identify patterns that help the teams I support. I need a routine. I struggle to function during the day when I am not settled into a routine.

The one truth I cling to is this: the disabilities that have shaped my struggles are also the source of my strength. The moniker, "disabled," is not one of defeat for me, but of joy, of proudly embracing the unique battles I've fought and the victories I've achieved. My experience, though at times isolating, has been the crucible from which empathy and understanding have emerged within me. It's equipped me with the tools to guide my children and nurture my students.

This book started because I was talking to a friend following a work call, and he asked me to tell him more about my story. He said that what I had to say was important. I expressed how difficult it is to write a long text, and he helped me write an initial outline. Yet, I found myself dealing with some significant anxiety about writing my story, and I hesitated to tell my husband, Robbi, despite his unwavering support.

It took me a while to articulate that it was not the idea of telling Robbi that made me nervous; it was not having control over how someone could use my story. I've spent a lifetime hearing people talk about me and people like me in the negative. I did not want my story used as a tool to say that all autistics look, act, and respond to life the way I do. I finally concluded that I do not have control over how others use my story, but if I do not write my story, I am not contributing to the many autistic, learning disability voices out there. I am adding to their silence. That is not ok with me.

I mustered the courage to reveal my plan to write a book to Robbi and shared a preliminary draft. As Robbi reviewed it for the first time, he remarked that I had initially written a mix of a memoir and a textbook, which was jarring to him as a reader. He suggested I provide more context about my personal story and less about the research and skills I gained along the way. He described something people have said to me for a long time: I tend to get technical. I go into a topic - any topic and I hyperfocus on details, and it's sometimes hard for me to see that people have drifted. I, however, see the gifts in the gap so I am motivated to investigate them and build solutions.

Robbi made me realize that I needed more self-awareness in both verbal and written communication. To provide context for this book, I had to delve into my childhood, recounting my school experiences and my subpar outcomes after high school graduation. It also involved sharing anecdotes about my children and students and the research, training, failures, and successes that have shaped my journey without diving face first into theory and data.

This memoir isn't just a personal narrative, it reflects how I perceive the world as an autistic person with learning disabilities, as Robbi pointed out. I've always sought logical patterns to understand my experiences - so this was not going to be an easy task. Generally, I rely on intellectualization, a trait often associated with individuals like me on the autism spectrum. My husband, who is not autistic, can separate his personal experiences from research and move forward. I'm sometimes jealous of his ability to do that, and I am learning that many people I know are similar to my husband. In my professional life, I have to do this consistently to understand coworkers. Researching and understanding patterns helps me do that.

This book describes how my children and I became literate and how I used the work we did to support my students when I became a special education teacher. Much research, testing, evaluation, and analysis went into this work. Unfortunately, when I first began researching learning disabilities in the United States as a doctoral student, and like my autism research, I encountered an overwhelming preponderance of studies centered around prison inmates or individuals confined to institutions. It's difficult to articulate the demoralization that comes with clicking through one link after another, only to find that researchers were viewing my community through the lens of the most damaging assumptions society held about us. The perspective of the research was often rooted in misperceptions of us as different or diminished, which stem from the consequences of the scarcity of resources available to us. My unsettling findings were compounded with another concern: my children and I were part of the disabled population, and the unacknowledged bias within the research projected a bleak outlook for us and others facing similar challenges.

Over time, my research journey unveiled a deeper understanding of the historical context underlying the exploration of learning disabilities. This exploration offered me valuable insights into the evolution of our collective knowledge. It paved the way for me to gain and share a more comprehensive perspective that acknowledges the diverse experiences and potentials of individuals with disabilities. I was able to see research expand from prison populations to classroom settings. Still, they were often narrated by others on behalf of our community. An example is a researcher identifying a group of "failing" students and discussing how different they were from higher-achieving students. They would then explain our deficits in detail and outline their solutions for support without having ever spoken to someone in our community to verify their assumptions. At times, I watched as they displayed individuals from our community in the worst light to support the solutions they were looking to present. Today, more people are speaking from within our community, and research is more inclusive and supportive of the disabled community.

Before you begin this book's first chapter, I need to dispel any notion that this journey was a walk in the park. I've often encountered biographies and personal accounts that portray individuals as possessing an almost supernatural resilience. However, I don't believe that's an accurate description of my story. I'm just an ordinary individual, standing at about five foot four inches in height, and sometimes my voice barely carries above a whisper.

I admit to being quite strict, often clinging to rules and guidelines. That is why my story is not the story of a flawless person with impeccably behaved children who conquered Mount Everest without encountering a single hurdle. No. There were challenges—plenty of them—many of which stemmed from my behavior. The amazing part is that learning about myself helped me to apologize where I needed to for the impact my disabilities had on them, and to clearly see where an apology from me was neither necessary, nor forthcoming. Reading this book means you will jump from a memoir to a textbook from time to time, and that's perfectly fine. It's not that I am intentionally attempting to tell my story in a confusing way. It is that I am trying to show what it's like to see the world through my eyes. My journey as a researcher and teacher is deeply intertwined with my autism, just as being Christian, Black, female, learning disabled, a wife, mother, daughter, sister, and friend are integral aspects of who I am. I can't escape or deny these identities. I'm grateful that Robbi helped me recognize my presence in this book and the need to explain it to those new to my experience.

What I hope you glean from this book is that you gain the capacity—regardless of how scant it may seem—to accomplish all that's required of you in due course. For any parent reading this book, our journey as parents is a marathon, not a sprint, and I'm sharing my journey with you because I feel that we are all obligated to one another to exchange our strategies and insights. Being illiterate was a roadblock that I thought I would never be able to overcome…BUT…God gave me a pencil!

I

THE EARLY YEARS

Though it's not the most significant thread in the tapestry of my story, it's crucial to note that I wasn't born into a lineage of educators or nestled within the cozy cocoon of academic pedigrees. My inception was in the urban embrace—a reality I share with countless others living in the heart of inner cities. My understanding of the inner city included small houses with many children, government cheese, charity food baskets, powdered milk, and many foster children. I traveled on a bus to schools outside my neighborhood, walked to a recreation center to play, and I spent a lot of time waiting for the streetlights to come on. My experience is founded in this locality, and though it may support a child who grew up in another setting, I did not live in any other space, so I do not pretend to speak from the lens of another person's experience.

I recognized my mother, Anne, by the smell of weed on her breath, the shape of her afro on her head, and her voice's weird pattern when she lied. She ate ice that she chipped by slamming it in a towel, cuddling it in her lap, spooning it into her mouth, and crunching it for hours. That day, she didn't crush ice. Her movements were jagged as she dressed us in brand new raincoats with hoods that had cartoon characters on them—red, yellow, and clear. We each got a tiny umbrella and matching boots. They were slick and sticky on my skin at the same time.

Rain drips slowly in the memory when combined with tears, the smell of urine, fear, pain, and regret. Fast drops in the sky and droplets on my sister's faces, around their eyes, or on their hair gather and roll delicately around to accentuate colors and details that I might ordinarily have missed. I'd never had anything new that I can remember—I'm sure I did, but I can't recall. One of my sisters was crying; she had already peed herself. I could smell plastic. My memory fades out until the image of us at the doorstep of my mom's friend. My mom begged her to take us; Mom would be back, she claimed. Bending, she kissed each of us. When she kissed me goodbye, she pulled back when I whimpered at the pain her lips caused my cheek and I covered my ears to stop the sound her lips made when they smacked together. Her friend, whose voice used to be pleasant, now had a bitter tone as she warned my mom not to take long. My mom's friend walked around me in her home, but she would yell at my sisters or touch them.

Eventually, the friend shuffled us inside and yelled at my sister, "You better not pee in my beds!" Pulling off our new clothes, her lips were thin as she grumbled angrily and yanked, then put us into a bath and bed for the night. My stomach hurt so much—I don't remember eating that day. I woke up beside my two sisters, wet with urine—a belt waiting to punish the sin. It didn't take long before my mom's friend got so angry that the spinning of the rotary dial phone began clicking back from each chosen number. Her voice turned frantic as her deep breaths altered the pattern of every word. She screamed for someone to hurry and slammed the headset down on the cradle with magnificent force. My mom had not returned, and my memory forbids me from knowing how long we had been there.

After the call, there's a blank space in my memory. When I wake up, I'm in a new place with new people. It's warm this time. I have a thing called a quilt wrapped around me. The food is warm, the milk a deep satin white— cool on my lips and the back of my throat. The woman has a kind voice and her house has soft lights. My sisters are out doing chores or riding horses. I was only separated from my sisters when they left in the morning to do chores, and there was a bitter, burning urine smell outside in the barn and around the animals. I wanted to do a chore, too, which I'd share with the kind woman. I had no idea what that was, but she took me out to a thing she called a chicken coup and told me to take the eggs from large birds. They pecked my hand, and that hurt. I hated those things, but I grabbed the eggs anyway because I wanted more than anything to be useful so that we could stay in that home. There were so many animals, and that was fascinating to my young mind. I had never seen animals (other than dogs or cats) before. What I liked about her was that she talked about forever homes as I swung my legs at the kitchen table, eating a meal. She had slower movements.

I was separated in my favorite foster home despite the house having calm voices and soft corners. I wish I had the memory to be as specific as I want to be. My sisters and I were within a year to two years of one another. I was inside most of the time and they were outside most of the time. People spoke to me using softer voices and they laughed more with my sisters. My sisters saw more of the farm; I only remember the chicken coop. I would not say I was lonely, though I was alone in the house or only with the kind woman. I saw my sisters after chores. There was no yelling until I was yelling, clinging to her as some stranger ripped me away from her.

The next thing I knew, I was jarred awake in a highchair with a bowl of brown puffy eyeballs in pale-colored milk staring back at me. The belt on the chair was painful because it pulled my skin tight. I could not twist out; it was hard to move, and my legs burned and tingled under the skin until they went numb from the pain. A woman with white skin (just like the kind woman) told me to eat. My sisters were just beyond a basement door frame behind a child's gate. *Why were they over there?* The woman's blue eyes were wild—her pupils pushing toward me like daggers because I didn't want to eat. There was so much yelling that I couldn't hear anymore. I only saw my sisters: short, tiny afros, huddled together behind that fence. When we were together, locked in a basement full of boxes, we were left to our own devices until, again, we were whisked away. The authorities placed us in the back of a car, drove us away from her, and reintroduced us to our maternal grandmother, Ethel, whom we called Grandma. I even remember being on one side of my grandmother on the plane home while my sisters were on the other side.

My sisters and I at our grandmother's house.

Our grandmother's haven was a four-bedroom home that sheltered not just me but a cacophony of siblings, cousins, and foster siblings. On the main floor of the house, I slept in a room with my grandmother, and two other children slept in the other room. Other foster siblings slept on blankets on the living room floor or in groups in the other two rooms upstairs; we were packed full. My clothes were hand-me-downs from Goodwill™ or purchased from the trunk of a car. Rarely we went to Payless™ to get a new pair of shoes.

Food came in large pans, deep enough to feed masses for a few days.

Kids stayed out of adult conversations and played outside until the streetlights came on. If you were allowed to be around adults, you did not make yourself noticeable. You listened because you had not yet earned the right to speak. There were no private spaces outside of the bathroom.

Amidst the hubbub, our grandmother stood tall with her fourth-grade education, imparting wisdom that transcended textbooks. She gave me as much as she could, and I am forever grateful for that, though I would come to understand that I'd need much more to succeed in life.

It's possible that the first indications of my disabilities were manifesting in these moments. I was not that different in age from my sisters, but people continued to separate us from one another. One might imagine it to be lonely, but it was more frightening. My sisters were the only people I had been with consistently, and I was prevented from being near them in nearly every setting. Our grandmother kept me close due to my behaviors. We were in different grades in school even though we walked together. They had friends they hung out with. At church, I was with the adult study group, and my sisters were in bible study class with other kids. It was like growing up together but apart.

No one in my life ever bent down to my face to tell me that I was the reason things were like they were—

but this was implied to me by the actions of the adults. I watched my sisters form a bond I never understood, beginning in my earliest memories. Don't misunderstand; my sisters were protective of me when they needed to be, but they always expressed that they felt I was spoiled when we were kids. They, too, were young, had been abused, and were hurting. Yet they were together in nearly every single moment. I never knew if it was due to the separation we experienced in the foster homes we were in, the separation we went through because of adult choices when we came back, or if it was due to their closeness in age. What I knew was that I always watched that from a distance.

I will never fully know what my mom was coping with. It's far too easy to try to make her a villain in my story, but in truth, she was a young person—a broken person—and she had a lot on her plate. I have no idea what she felt or experienced as she raised us. I do not know if my behavior drove her to leave us. My memory only allows me to see the results of my actions on others. It does not afford me the ability to know my true impact.

I observed my impact on adults all around me. The woman feeding me in the highchair would slam her fist on the table when I tried to close my mouth from the spoon. That same woman pulled the belt on the highchair tight, locking me in so completely that I could not escape.

As a child, when connecting with my siblings proved difficult, I found myself seeking refuge in the company of adults. The subtle yet obvious sounds of deep sighs with hand swipes across the foreheads or faces of adults filled my childhood. So did the sight of tight fists with large veins popping out of them and turning heads and whispering between adults.

If I did spend time with other children (who were not my oldest sisters), I found the experience draining and difficult. My solace came from watching television.

Unbeknownst to me, this electronic companion would become my first teacher—it helped me to understand what people thought; there was often a narrator or the characters would have external dialogues about their internal worlds. This stark contrast between screen and reality ignited an internal dissonance that deepened as I grew older.

One of my other major struggles was with definitions—people changed definitions so much that they became a baffling dance where words were framed and reframed without adhering to any consistent meaning but instead connected to body language, culture, or innuendo that was commonly shared by people who understood social cues that I didn't understand then, and am still learning to understand now.

This period haunts me. There was so much that I didn't understand. No one's actions matched their words. My mom said she would be back, but she never returned to get us. Her friend said she loved us, but she yelled because we were in her house. The woman with the brown, puffy eyeball cereal said she would take all three of us, but she separated us from one another or hid us in the basement. The kind woman talked about forever homes, but they took us from her, so this period haunts me. People never said what they meant, and in my tiny mind, this meant that people were liars.

It wasn't just the meaning of words or social language that failed to line up for me. It was also touch; physical connection bore its own language, and this language felt filled with lies too. People in real life touched each other, and the touch had its own meaning. Yet, touch from others brought me a wave of discomfort, a torrent of fatigue that coursed through my body like lightning in a powerful storm. Strangely enough, my family seemed to understand this phenomenon. They sensed my unease and comprehended that touching wasn't soothing but, in fact, was distressing. My grandmother was one of the few people that I touched without hesitating inside of my head.

Looking back, I understand more of my siblings' challenges when dealing with me. I was a rigid, complex, withdrawn child. I rarely understood when to laugh at a joke, I struggled to engage in play with others, and I clung to a specific set of rules that guided my actions. This wasn't their fault or mine—it simply was. I can't imagine how they would describe growing up with me. This is one reason why it is so vital to me that I don't share this in a way that stigmatizes them. My parents and siblings had their own personal battles (my father had bipolar disorder), and I had no right to expect them to fully understand or cope with who I was at the time, or how I am now as an adult, because I did not understand them either. The same goes for my friends. I indicated before that people joke about things, often the things that scare them. Because disabilities can lead to a significant lack of resources, I don't think anyone wants that for the people they love, so they guard against it by acting like it does not exist.

Before coming to live in our grandmother's home full time, my two older sisters and I had moved constantly. We had no experience with stable living environments, so my transition to preschool vividly stands out. Transitions were hard – they still are. This transition moved me from the chaos of our grandmother's home to a consistently calm environment where I could experiment.

I recall the sensory experience of mixing peanuts in butter to craft a type of peanut butter for sandwiches. I staked my claim to a small, tiny human-sized mat, a personal sanctuary settled in the farthest darkest corner of the dimly lit classroom—a room that seemed tailor-made for my small self. My food was my own, and it came in mini sizes where sharing was not permitted, and everyone had equal portions.

I loved being in that space, but I hated the playground. I was separated from my siblings and pushed in with other children my age, many of them with ulterior motives. That space felt dangerous, especially if you were caught by yourself. I was anxious for the bell to ring to bring us back into the classroom.

Preschool and kindergarten were peaceful to me outside of the playground.

Two years later, life orchestrated a shift—a move to a new neighborhood—and my comfort zone was shattered. A new house, an unfamiliar yard, a community filled with strangers, more kids, and even more social settings to learn. All of it was unpredictable! My sisters and I were destined to be bused—a notion entirely foreign to me—to schools farther away. My grandmother gave me directions of northwest corners and cardinal points without landmarks. My compass seemed hopelessly skewed, my choices were gone, and I had no option but to fall in line.

Somehow, the first day of first grade feels like it was yesterday. We set out in the early morning, the sun high enough that yellow light burned my open eyes. I put my head down and took one step at a time along the concrete sidewalk. I barely heard the instructions on where to go and knew I didn't understand them anyway. I had on white shoes and dark blue jeans. I remember picking out those shoes. They had tiny, even little holes in them on both sides. The holes formed a nice pattern. My grandmother was furious that the pair had cost $14.99 when I could have had two pairs for $10.99. Our store limit that day was $10.99. But I didn't budge. I wanted those shoes, refused to try others on, and wanted socks that didn't poke. That was another $2.49. In a house with so many children, that was a lot to afford, but she did buy them.

That morning, however, I took a breath with each step that took me away from home. I was careful not to step on cracks or lines and nearly tripped a few times. As we neared the bus stop, I looked up long enough to notice the bus was not there yet. A feeling of isolation enveloped me—a bubble grew in my chest, and my focus constricted. The pressure within my ears intensified, verging on pain.

I tried to move closer to my siblings, but they were conversing with other kids. I hadn't noticed the kids until then. Once we got on the bus, I sat in front of my sisters. I heard one of my siblings say, "Don't touch her. She hates that." And then came the touch—a single light touch to the back of my neck that raised the hairs. It triggered a cascade of reactions. It drained my emotional energy while fueling a physically impulsive response that marked my first suspension in grade school and ruined those white shoes that my grandmother had spent so much money on. In my memory, this is the time when touch transformed from a tortuous gesture that I simply hated into a spiteful bullying tactic, as one little boy used it to push me to fight so often that I lost morning outdoor privileges for first and second grade and developed an unexpected companionship with my first-grade teacher, Ms. Maze. She was a remarkable woman who opted to keep me in her class by volunteering to teach me in the second grade.

I will never know if she had any idea that I was autistic. I was not tested for disabilities then, but she dimmed the lights in the classroom and allowed me to sit by myself and play games with marbles or strings while she read in the front of the classroom without engaging with me. I sat in the same seat for two years, and I was not expected to sit in the middle of small groups when she called everyone to the front of the room. She provided me with a spot on the edges. No one could be in my space. Without knowing it, she had created the same conditions in her room as my preschool and kindergarten classrooms.

But she also removed me entirely from social engagement in the mornings with a plan to gradually allow me to have that privilege back if I earned it. The boy who picked on me never lost the privilege of being outside with other students. And this is part of the beginning of how I was marginalized. It's the marker I reach back to that told me in no uncertain terms that I was different. The teacher's action reminded me that the world was not made to my specifications and that I would be punished if I didn't learn to fit in. I started using masking, though unintentionally, to guard myself. Masking is crafting a daily disguise; it's an artful way of concealing or downplaying one's authentic self, emotions, abilities, disabilities, or struggles. It's a way of wearing an invisible mask not for celebration but to seamlessly merge into the background, to discourage undue attention and avoid the spotlight. This is where I began masking. As the word implies, I assumed invisible disguises to try to conform to the classroom environment and others' behaviors.

II

STIGMA

"Wisdom calls out in the street;
she makes her voice heard in the public squares.
She cries out above the commotion:
she speaks at the entrance of the city gates."
Proverbs 1: 20-21 (CSB)

In the late 1970s and early 1980s, nestled in the grandeur of the Rocky Mountains, Denver, Colorado, was undergoing a profound metamorphosis, which echoed through the city's streets and the mountain landscape beyond. The economy, once tethered to mining and farming, was becoming more entwined with the energy industry. This dynamic shift breathed new vitality into Denver's economy, and the city's population surged as people were drawn by the allure of new opportunities against the backdrop of the Rockies.

Growing up in Denver during this era, my experience intertwined with the changing fabric of the city. The neighborhoods of Denver, including Park Hill, where we lived, displayed the ebb and flow of cultural shifts, economic changes, and changing social dynamics. The city was experiencing the ripple effects of national events (integrated busing, redline racial zoning in urban communities, and the war on drugs), from economic recessions to political upheavals, all of which influenced the lives of Denver's inhabitants, young and old.

I had a few teachers who presumed I (we - the students) needed to fully understand the dynamics of the city I (we) lived in. Yet I had my own problems and didn't care much about the city around me. I didn't really understand or experience changes outside of my own home. Until I met my grandmother's boss, I thought everyone in my neighborhood lived the same way. I lived with a matriarch. We had family in every corner of the house. Cousins, siblings, foster kids, visiting neighbors, and family members constantly gathered. I knew that my family used government assistance because I was with my grandmother when she went to pick up commodities, also known as government-assisted food.

We ate thick bologna and cheese sandwiches and sometimes meat that came in a can. I ate Farina™ from the government. It came in a white box with big dark brown or black letters. On TV, those boxes from which smiling children poured cereal were red with a picture of a man and a bowl on the cover, but ours were different. Butter came in brick-like blocks, and we got cereal from the grocery aisle with inch-thick, white and black twisted strings at the top of it. I knew we were poor because of where we shopped for clothes and how we paid bills—money orders, no checks, sometimes cash.

What we did not have was access to the world outside of our own understanding. Many things were out of our reach, so we learned to make do with what we had. I often wonder if that is where my tenaciousness came from. Lack, in and of itself, is an influential teacher. I may have missed skills I needed throughout my life without it.

From elementary to high school, I navigated the challenges of undiscovered, unnamed learning disabilities and personal obstacles the best way I could at the time—without knowing I was struggling more than anyone else or how things would turn out.

In terms of physicality, I always seemed to be just a step behind my peers. With a lanky frame and a bit on the shorter side, I was a thin silhouette amid the crowd. This was not a wonderful thing in my home. Women in my culture were supposed to be shapely with beautiful brown skin—darker than mine. Women who laughed loudly could hold their own on the streets, and women ran everything.

Too much time spent in front of the television screen had me inadvertently imitating cultures and styles that weren't quite in sync with my surroundings. My peers said I spoke like white people, but I only thought I talked like me. I carried books because that's what I thought you were supposed to have in school. No matter how much I tried, I never understood how people could show up at school and understand after hearing something once.

I knew it was dangerous when we lived on Denver's east side because we (my foster siblings, cousins, birth siblings and I) walked in packs. We went to events as a group. We were not out after dark. I knew when my favorite person (a cousin whom I loved) died, and I knew because we talked about drug addiction in my home. I slept in my grandmother's room, so I woke up for emergencies and listened intently to the bad things happening to the family, neighborhood friends, and others who visited my grandmother in the middle of the night.

When we first moved to Park Hill, it was peaceful, even though I didn't handle the transition well. We had more grass to play on, and I could walk to the park alone. I could see the stars brightly in the sky. I could watch the clouds form shapes when I lay on a blanket in the park. Things changed again when gangs (Crips and Bloods) began infesting Denver neighborhoods, which eventually led to the Summer of Violence in 1993. We didn't stay up late lying on pallets in the middle of the living room with the front door open anymore. Violence consumed nearly every space. Rapes, shootings, and drugs were much closer than before. As a result, instead of sitting on quilts and blankets at the front door and staring at the stars, we were in before dark. Neighbors went from trusting one another to keeping to themselves.

While city violence was increasing, threatening my sense of physical safety, I continued masking my true self at school, trying to achieve and keep some sense of intellectual safety. I learned more and more sophisticated ways to mask my learning disabilities, grasping for power over my situation.

Spelling tests—one per week, every week— a regular feature of my schooling journey, carried their own weight of anxiety. By the time fourth grade rolled around, I'd honed a ritual: I wrote down the word lists ten times daily from Monday to Thursday, with one last session on Friday morning. It was a strategy that allowed me to ace the tests, even when the words slipped away from my memory by the following Monday.

Sometimes, though, we were made to line up right before the test and to spell the words aloud in random order. I had only remembered the order we wrote them in each Monday. Oh, the shame and mortification that would wash over me when I inadvertently spelled a word wrong, especially when it sounded uncannily similar to another word (like flower and flour)! I'd hang my head and my shoulders would slump, leaving me with leaden feet and clouded vision for the rest of the day.

My fourth grade teacher threw compound and combined words into the mix. In my understanding, that meant instead of grappling with ten words, I had to tackle a whopping twenty. One morning, by some stroke of luck, I managed to evade the standing spelling quiz, positioning myself for the written exam instead. I remember the paper vividly—half a page with those delicate blue lines forming rows and a lone red line gracing the left-hand side. I meticulously sharpened my two trusty #2 pencils, gently spinning them in the pencil sharpener until the wood gave way to the blades. The satisfying sound of the sharpening process lingered as I carefully carried them back to my desk.

When the teacher handed me the paper, I printed my name, the class, the teacher's name, the date, numbered each row from one to ten, aligned the paper next to my pencils, sat up tall in my seat, and folded my arms neatly on the table. My teacher reviewed the test rules, and with each word, he recited a sentence. I etched out each letter in cursive, forming the words with precision. For the first time, I felt a surge of absolute confidence in my correctness. Upon completing the task, I submitted my paper, offered a smile in the direction of my teacher, and settled back into my seat with a sense of pride. After the test, the class lined up to move on to the next subject down the hall. I inhaled deeply, awaiting whatever was to follow. Standing in line, the class waited for the other teacher to open the door. It was then that I heard yelling in the hall.

"Are you trying to be a smart aleck?"

In the blink of an eye, the students fell silent and I could hear pounding footsteps heading in our direction.

Before I knew it, my teacher whirled me around. His grip tightened around my shoulders as he shook me violently, his voice booming in my face. He accused me of intentionally acting out, declaring I'd done it on purpose. But I had no idea what he meant.

He marched me down to the principal's office, where he engaged in a tense conversation with the principal. They left me waiting in the main office, my heart racing with bewilderment, my shoulders still feeling the pressure of his fingers on my skin. The principal eventually approached, his tone kind as he asked if I understood what I'd done wrong. I shook my head, genuinely clueless. He then asked me to spell *pirate ship*, and I did so confidently—out loud and accurately. Yet, his demeanor remained stern. "That's not what you wrote," he stated matter-of-factly. "Regardless, you're going to be suspended."

He slid the paper across the desk so I could see it. Tears welled up as I stared at my writing. I had ended *ship* with a "t" instead of a "p." The weight of the moment pressed down, and all I could do was cry. I hadn't done it intentionally but was destined for trouble anyway.

Around that time, my grandmother arrived, her expression a mix of concern and something I couldn't quite decipher. She questioned me about the situation, and I spilled out every detail. There was a momentary exchange of glances between her and the principal before they instructed me to wait in the hallway. My grandmother emerged, reassuring me that I wasn't in trouble but that I'd spend a few days away from school and return to a different class.

I later learned that my old teacher had been removed due to his inappropriate behavior toward me that day. Yet no one ever asked me to explain my understanding of how the situation had unfolded or why I struggled to spell the same words correctly just a week later. The enduring impression I carried away from that episode was that I should remain silent. Mistakes were unacceptable and stirred up disturbances. Above all, I should recognize that my voice often bounced against a brick wall unless it involved someone other than myself.

As grade school ended, I found myself dealing with a disheartening reality. Much of the information I was exposed to in the classroom remained elusive to me. Crafting coherent sentences on paper was an uphill battle, and stringing paragraphs together felt like an intricate puzzle I couldn't entirely solve. My ability to mimic, however, was growing more refined. I had stumbled upon several makeshift tools to navigate the academic maze, albeit imperfectly.

I created other survival techniques, writing vocabulary words with chopped sentences from different books to form poems, carrying pounds of books to feign having a literary interest. One of my strategies involved seeking refuge in the library. I'd approach the librarian, requesting books that aligned with the topics covered in class. When faced with a writing assignment, I would piece together sentences from these books, forming a patchwork paper that sometimes resembled a list of disjointed thoughts. A subpar grade seemed preferable to a zero.

I also began copying my textbooks cover to cover, an arduous task that I hoped would grant me an edge. As teachers lectured, I'd watch for the page they projected onto the screen, noting its progress in the book. I carefully folded the corner of the corresponding page in my copied textbook. The promise of open-book and open-notes tests became my lifeline, with the correct answer just a page flip away.

However, during my seventh-grade year, my approach caught the discerning eye of a teacher who sensed something was wrong. She took me aside for a conversation and administered a straightforward test. I don't remember all the details of the conversation she and I had together. She led me to a room and had me answer a few questions on a paper and she verbally asked me some things. This assessment resulted in me being led to the principal's office (again), where a call was placed to my grandmother.

When the school could not convince my grandmother to have me tested for a disability, those "assessments" I had taken somehow convinced my teachers to put me through a string of other tests that my grandmother did not know about. They did not have the right to test me. My grandmother was never informed. I was never told the results. I was removed from class for several days and sat in a classroom with just a teacher. After those tests, they had me sit with someone as they selected my class schedule for 9th grade and had me sign the enrollment paperwork. I really did not understand what I was about to enter into. Many of the classes I could not pronounce. All of this took place before the No Child Left Behind (NCLB) and other changes in special education took place in 2002. Based on those "tests", I was placed in some pretty heavy courses (physics, algebra 2, and geometry). I could not explain anything on the tests and had no idea what the questions asked, but whatever I put down convinced them that I was smart enough to take courses whose names I struggled to pronounce, let alone read at that time.

It was at this time that the word "dyslexia" first entered my consciousness, and it also was the first time my grandmother explained why she did not want me tested. She told me that I was not stupid and she did not want me in classes with certain kids. It was a perplexing twist of fate. I knew I was failing my current classes, yet I somehow managed to receive passing grades and be placed into more advanced classes.

I got tested but was trapped. I did not understand that they had no right to do that to me. I did not know the tests they gave me led to my enrollment in classes that were way above my head and reading level. I did not select or sign-off on those classes because I wanted them. I had to just accept it and move on, and my grandmother revealed how me being labeled with a disability was a bad thing in her eyes.

People were moving me from one challenging situation to another, indifferent to the weight of depression, anxiety, and frustration that I carried on my shoulders. Day after day, I showed up, acutely aware of my struggles and aching for support that remained elusive. I had to keep my head low, not get caught being distracted, and act like I understood even when I didn't. After my seventh grade teacher, no other teacher asked if I could read, they never corrected the things I wrote, and math was all multiple choice.

The stress added to the pressure of being found out and unmasked, and I began looking for any avenue of escape. Not even one teacher held me accountable; several stated in class, "No matter what happens in my class, you will never get below a C grade." That told me in no uncertain terms that all I had to do was make it to the building, and I would graduate from high school. It felt like there were no adults who cared about my situation. They had no idea how scared I was because I could not navigate the world and they were not providing me the appropriate skills.

There was one other who saw through my guise. Her name is Latifah. Latifah has been my best friend since I was a sophomore in high school. When other people assumed that I could read and write, Latifah didn't. I officially met her in geometry class.

Latifah noticed when I would show up to school inebriated, or she would look at my papers and see that I had not marked anything. She would glare at me, click her tongue, snatch my paper, and answer for me.

I was coping. School was difficult for me and I hated being there. My stress was high, and I didn't have the words to express that to anyone. None of my siblings or the other foster kids were like me; that was clear. I struggled to get the right words out like me; that was clear. I struggled to get the right words out and that impacted my overall communication. Teachers in high school had their own agendas and were not listening to students. I was looking for a way to just bury the fear that was inside of me.

Eventually, Latifah tried to tutor me in geometry, but I struggled to remember anything beyond her sessions. It bothered her, but she always told me I was smart enough to do anything. Latifah did know one thing about me: I loved God. I could never fully describe why I had faith, especially when I acted as I did. While we sat in her attic bedroom, I always had my Bible with me, but I wasn't not reading it. I had spent lots of time scanning the pages for text I had highlighted when we went over it in church, but I was not really reading it; I was learning to memorize what was repeated.

This infuriated her. She demanded to know how I could say I had faith in a God that I had not read about. I told her that despite everything, I had seen evidence of God in my life, and she said that was not good enough, that I could not defend my faith if I could not read. She then asked me if I had read Revelation (for those with no idea, it's the last book of the Bible). I said no. Latifah then gave me my first true reading lesson using the book where my faith would be grounded.

I may have already been connected with Latifah, but this kindness bonded me to her and my God for life. I learned that day that the end of the book was just as fascinating as the beginning and not as scary as people had made it seem. In one afternoon, she helped me accomplish something I never thought possible: I finished something I started. I remembered some of it, and even though she yelled at me, I never felt shame or humiliation. Latifah and I would grow to believe in different religions, but our friendship remained. Latifah has supported me through every significant event in my life. Her determination to make me read gave me the resolve to build and rebuild my life. She is forever my best friend and sister, and I thank God for her every time I think about her.

In my early adulthood, I began working for Colorado UpLift and I found myself in the role of a classroom teacher. The organization's novelty worked in my favor, allowing me to rely on shared wisdom from elders rather than solely on my personal knowledge. Whenever my verbal, writing, or reading limitations were at risk of being exposed, I deflected by attributing my errors to a lack of preparation time or by presenting information I was pretending to study. When I did admit my lack of understanding, my masking efforts inadvertently obscured the true impact of my condition, hindering others' ability to help me.

It's weird to explain to others, but the masking required in my house differed from the masking required in my neighborhood, which differed from the masking I had to do in each classroom setting, at church, in youth groups, and on various jobs. Every entity was a different culture with one connecting tie: They all had stigmas about disabilities. There was a learning curve in every setting, and exposure was always on my mind. I couldn't be my most authentic self, and I was missing the connection with people who have a similar understanding. So, I acted the part in every setting, hoping that no one figured it out. This is a veiled struggle. It increased stress, depression, and anxiety, which could already be elevated, depending on the situation.

I was exhibiting signs and symptoms of my condition, but because I was masking, I had, in fact, forced myself into being functionally (problems with reading and writing as an adult) and culturally (problems being able to communicate with people in my own culture) illiterate. My autism, my faith, and my need for rules, regulations, and structure helped me in the area of moral literacy (the ability to apply ethics, reason and use moral imagination), but my ability to understand morality got firmly in the way of my cultural awareness. It was the reason I was so rigid that I could not conform to certain cultural norms. The more I masked, the more difficult it became for others to notice my challenges, for me to face the social stigma associated with my challenges, and for me to get help from a professional. I wanted help. I wanted to learn. I even wanted to go to college.

I remember the one time I visited a college campus as a high school student. I saw students wandering the small university campus learning a trade—something I wanted but could not understand how to get. I imagined being one of those students, truly learning, and having confidence in a skill. It was the first time I truly ever wanted to be part of a learning community. I didn't care about the green grass, the dormitories, the cafeteria, or the quiet atmosphere (which was new for me). I found myself craving to be with different people and cultures and learning to think differently. I wanted to understand the ins and outs of new opportunities, and I wanted to benefit from what I would be learning. I began to imagine myself on campus, and that was scary.

Throughout my life, I was told by people I loved that obtaining a higher degree was out of my reach, or that going to college proved that I didn't want to be part of my own culture and assumed I thought I was better than the people I grew up with. The hard truth was that I envied the people I grew up with because most of them knew and understood their purpose. That gave them confidence and helped them stand tall in my eyes. I could only mimic their confidence because I didn't have it for myself. People in my neck of the woods went to trade school, so I thought I would give that a try. Unfortunately, I struggled to remember anything I learned, which meant I was unable to take the state test that was required at the end of that training. I had gone through an entire year of classes, writing things down, listening to try to understand, and it was all gone. I told others that it was the cost of the test, but it was my lack of recall that hindered me.

Colorado UpLift attempted to help me go to college the first time. The skills I used successfully to mask during work hours failed me in the college classroom. Within two years, I had to drop out because I was failing, which left me with debt, more significant depression, and discouragement. In protecting myself, I was failing myself, and that's a reality that I live with daily.

Growing up, I was always told that I would follow in my grandmother's footsteps as a matriarch, or I'd get married and take care of my own family as a homemaker. I had no idea that I had other options. One of my siblings branched out and became a beautician; I was so proud of her. Yet I had no idea how she negotiated public spaces to learn that such an option was there. Public schools at the time taught subjects like crafts, home economics, woodshop, etc. Short of sewing shirts or pillows I'd never use again and baking horrendous cookies, the information never translated into a career plan, not to mention that I typically forgot as much as I learned at that time. Really, I learned to cook at home, but that only translated, in my mind, to cooking for a large family. I'm not sure I have ever learned how to cook for fewer than seven people.

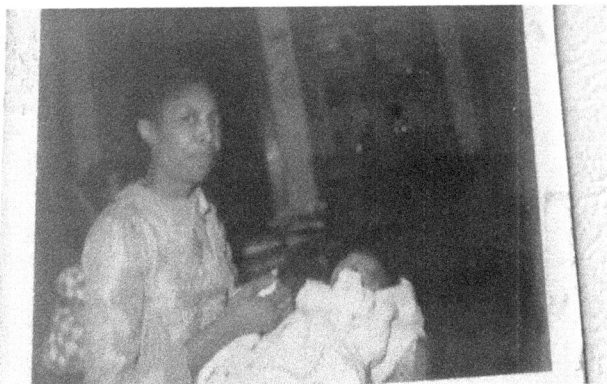

My grandmother holding me as a baby.

I had been able, from a young age, to go to work with my grandmother, who was a maid for a local attorney. By thirteen, I got a small job copying documents by hand at a local medical center. I earned money for a time as a youth counselor through a program my church was connected to, and Colorado UpLift hired me to mentor students at a local middle school. I was able to intern at various places over my summers. Most of the tasks I performed did not require writing. Many of the jobs required some type of childcare, which I'd been doing at home, so I had experience there.

As soon as a task required reading or writing, I needed support, even when completing a job application. Employers presumed that questions on a job application were simple, but I was negotiating spelling, names of streets I'd lived on, names of people I worked with, and the exact dates of when I worked at various places. All of these were things I struggled to remember, especially when I felt pressured. I used to think, *Why can't I just walk in, watch someone do the task I'd be hired to do, mimic the task, and earn the paycheck?* It's not easy for me to admit that I was ashamed and angry with the entire process. All I wanted to do was earn my own way and live in a small home.

When I was working for a local medical office, I got in trouble for the number of mistakes I made trying to copy text onto three layers of Medicaid paperwork. I'd start one word and mistakenly write another. This forced me to restart multiple times until the task was completed. Unfortunately, because I was moving word by word and sometimes not working fast enough for the office, my job was in jeopardy. I began coming in about an hour earlier and hiding in the back part of the office to get as much done as possible before the staff came in. Any mistakes were torn to pieces, placed into a dark paper sack, and tossed in the alley trash. Alphabetizing was difficult because everything had to be in order by last name and then by first name. I had to line up every paper/file and sing the alphabet in my head over and over until the documents were in the correct order. Then I would file them. By the end of the summer, I was exhausted. I felt ashamed and helpless.

During my internship at a local bank, attention to detail was also key. Any debris in the paperwork could break or temporarily shut down the microfiche machine. Removing debris was cumbersome; it required bending over a desk for hours, moving large tubs to and from rooms, and catching mistakes on the back end. Part of my job was to catch misfiled documents and send them back to someone higher up to review. This was difficult for me because I could not read much of what was on the page.

There is something about black text on white paper that my eyes struggle with. I find myself feeling fatigued, passing out, and retracing lines to understand what is written. Luckily, documents that might need review had a specific picture on them. No matter what the document said, I played it safe and sent everything with that picture back. I was scolded a few times, but I just reiterated it was not my job to determine importance. It was only my job to refer it back. I had a great coworker; she had been with the company for a long time, and she caught things I missed on more than one occasion.

My position was not needed by the end of the summer, so even though my back was in severe pain, and I would have been willing to continue in the position, the opportunity was short-lived. I was about 100-105 pounds soaking wet and the tubs holding the paper were heavy as I lugged them across the office and then had to bend over them to remove the contents.

The opportunities I had gave me priceless life skills that helped me to build a strong work ethic. Yet I wanted something more in life. Not that these jobs were not good jobs. I learned that every job is important, but I wanted something sustainable that made me want to come to work every morning and supported my personal talents and strengths. The problem was, I did not know or understand how to figure out what those were.

People say you can be anything you want to be in life, but these people know their talents, their skills, and they have some idea of their value in the workplace, giving them something to strive for. They never tell you how hard you might have to work to get there. When I had no idea what I brought to the table, employers took advantage of me as a warm body, which pierced my heart and created bitterness at work.

III

SKILLS,
SKILLS, SKILLS

"Do you see a person skilled in his work?
He will stand in the presence of kings.
He will not stand in the presence of unknown men."
Proverbs 22: 29 (HCSB)

1991 was an interesting year. I needed to have a good income if I was ever going to find a place to live outside of my grandmother's house. I had talked to one of my sisters about finding a trade and she directed me to look at business schools. There was a business school nearby called Mansfield Business College, and they had certified nursing assistant (CNA) programs, which I decided to try. For $6,000, I got all my books and registered to take several classes each day. No one told me the specifics of the paperwork I was signing; the loan officer just told me where to sign and gave some idea of how much the loans would be.

Once the paperwork was complete, the financial aid office walked me to a room that had piles and piles of books. They handed me a stack of books and told me where my classes would be. I was in complete shock. My sister had taken classes, and I never recalled seeing any textbooks (though I'm sure I just spaced out that part of her learning). I thought all the work was hands-on, like the required typing classes. How on earth was I going to complete a class? I'd only made it through high school because most of my teachers gave me a C just for showing up to class. Now, someone was telling me that to change bedpans or support nurses, I had to actually read and understand math! It felt impossible.

I started writing every single note that teachers put on the board but was too embarrassed to ask them to stop when I was getting behind. I would indicate to myself that I missed notes by writing three dots at the end of statements. I got through exams, but the information was gone the next day or the following week. I could not identify the content when the exams were over.

I loved my patients, however. Spending time during my lunch hour at the bedside of a lonely patient whose family didn't show up made me feel like I had some purpose, but nurses in the field thought I was getting too close to patients, particularly my elderly patients. I wasn't; many had no idea I was in the room. Most of their rooms were quiet. Sitting with patients could be more peaceful than sitting in the cafeteria, and some just told stories without engaging me in conversation. Still, I was told on several occasions by other nurses that if I could not separate myself from my patients I was not going to last in the field.

What they did not understand was that I knew I would never pass the CNA exam. I could barely remember what I needed to know to pass the shorter exams each week. The patients needed and deserved someone they could depend on, someone who could read and catch mathematical errors. Lives were at stake. I had enough compassion for my patients that I knew the risk I posed to them was not worth it. The financial and tangible costs of my illiteracy were clear to me then; I had to find a solution or I was going to fail myself.

In the fall of 1992, I was working for Colorado UpLift. I knew I was going to have to begin paying back my loans for the Mansfield CNA program, and I was only making a tiny salary of $64.00 bi-weekly. The same year, one of the donors of that organization decided to provide two scholarships for employees to attend school. I was one of the recipients. Regardless of the scholarship, however, the school required my grandmother's private social security information and my personal financial information. For me to receive financial aid, Mansfield never required those; I just signed on the dotted line. After hearing what the college wanted, my grandmother refused and was furious that I would even ask, if, after all, someone else was paying for it.

Following a series of meetings with the school's financial aid office, I had to file for independent status, complete a college application, and write an essay. I still did not understand what FAFSA meant or all of the details of the paperwork. I did not have the skill set to comprehend the questions. I was confused. I had to learn something to survive, so I didn't have a choice; I had to pretend to understand and sign my name on the dotted line.

The school didn't allow me to go home or the library to write the required essay. I had to sit down outside the office and put my thoughts on paper about how I planned to be an excellent student. Again, I failed to understand how this was important; I was there to learn a skill I didn't have. I felt that the essay would be more important after I'd learned whatever it was that the school planned to teach me, but I wrote the essay. I think the registrar scanned it, filed it, and welcomed me to school.

The scholarship was somehow not enough to cover books or room and board. I would have to travel to school on the bus for two hours in each direction while working full-time at UpLift. I slept roughly four hours a night at most. Because I could not afford all of my school books (something that is still puzzling to me), I needed to rise early enough to get to the library when it opened, and I bought as many spiral notebooks as I could afford. There was a lot of copying I was going to need to do since scanning texts cost five cents per page — an additional cost I could not afford.

I was required to take four classes each semester to remain in good standing with financial aid and keep my current loans in forbearance, and I had to maintain good grades to keep the scholarship. Hoping to start things as simply as possible, I started with some acting, creative arts, and a history class. My church had us doing skits as teenagers, and I didn't think this would be any different. I discovered on day one that I was in over my head. The acting classes required reading large passages and remembering them while being on stage. I don't know why it never occurred to me that performance would be involved; it just never did. I had to find monologues on my own and pretend in front of others; I was in deep trouble, and I knew it.

Things took a more painful turn when, after a fight in my home, I found myself wandering the streets of Denver, trying to figure out where I was going to live. It was the first time in my life that I had ever been homeless and alone. I wandered downtown Denver for hours, evaluating the possibility of places I saw from the safety of the city bus. These familiar settings suddenly felt haunted. I was ashamed to ask for help. I knew what it was like to be poor, but I had no idea how I was going to navigate life with no place to stay. *What was I going to eat?* I had just a few dollars and some change in my pocket. Knowing I had to get to work that first night, I went to a payphone and called my mentor to pick me up. I prayed pretty hard, and thanked God that people took pity on me and allowed me to couch-hop for about a month.

I had to take out additional loans for the school to allow me to move to campus, and I thought that would give me a chance to save a few hours a day and study. I'd never lived with people of another culture before. I grew up not understanding the social norms of my own culture, and now I had to live with people who were very different. Additionally, I had to figure out how to purchase items for daily living—soap, towels, blankets. I had nothing, but needed money for everything; even though I got loans and a scholarship, basic necessities were not covered. I could not find the logic there. I had to take my entire $64 paycheck and spend it on food and incidentals. A boyfriend purchased my glasses (they were expensive), and I tried life on campus in a brand new culture. Again, I found myself floundering.

Illiteracy is dangerous because it steals hope. It nearly stole mine. No matter how many notes I took or conversations I had in class, I was not retaining information. I'd tried going out with friends to ease the tension. After one long night out, I was assaulted in a vehicle and struggled to escape the overwhelming sense of fear that came over me.

I was not a stranger to that type of violence, but this instance was different. I was more vulnerable than ever because of the changes I had gone through when I left home and moved to the college campus, scrambling to pay for everything and working my way through my classes. I knew that I had limited options at the time, and this situation broke me. Because of the assault, the stress that I had been under to find a life for myself torched suddenly, stripping me down to my very core. I could not study. I could not think. I was afraid everywhere I went. My anxiety reached such a height that I could not bring it down.

I went on a drinking bender for three days. I felt hopeless, depressed, and withdrawn. It's hard to describe the depth of uncertainty that I had.

My last hope was to go back to my grandmother. I had to rely on my family for my basic survival because I was desperate. During this time, I experienced life-altering events such as becoming a mother, getting married the first time, and subsequently divorcing. Through these changes, I had to learn to scour newspapers for phrases like "paid training" in hopes of finding potential opportunities. I made a conscious effort to present myself well for interviews, yet my grasp of what I learned remained fleeting.

One of the jobs I secured was with a company affiliated with America Online™. In my new role, I became acquainted with a remarkable individual named Daniel Embry. He generously dedicated his mornings to guiding me through the intricacies of answering calls for the helpdesk. With his unwavering support and patience, I transitioned from assisting the public at the tier 1 help desk—resolving computer screen errors—to the soft skills support desk. In this latter role, I participated in crafting materials to train our phone staff in effective call-handling techniques. A group of us sat and listened to recorded phone calls and troubleshot solutions to help the staff stop problematic behaviors. This was great because we talked about solutions and tested a few things before we wrote them down.

This was a time predating widespread internet access. Consequently, I lacked access to a wealth of training resources. Instead, I shared what I had learned from Daniel when I started the job with the team. I found a professional development plan at the office, and we used it to create a curriculum with a phone script, albeit one that was laden with spelling and grammatical errors. I attributed the sloppy nature of my work to the urgency of the task and lack of time I had at home to complete my additional work, given my personal circumstances. My life was tumultuous at that point. I was trying to get away from my ex and was a single mother, taking numerous bus rides to transport my daughter and myself. My appearance likely mirrored the chaos of my life, and with a salary of approximately $9 per hour, I was teetering on the edge of losing my only state benefit: childcare support.

My daughter faced her own health battles, including chronic illnesses like asthma, eczema, and severe allergies. My primary resources included my job, the occasional assistance from state-provided commodities, basic office supplies like pens and paper, and the generosity of friends. Financial stability eluded me, a situation shared by many in my community, and my inability to manage finances, establish social connections, access higher-paying job opportunities, or effectively navigate the complex medical landscape in the Denver Metro area on behalf of my daughter profoundly impacted my life's trajectory.

I eventually secured a position at US West™, a telecommunications company that offered employees educational reimbursement opportunities. I did want a college education, even though I failed the last time. I tried to tell myself I had new skills this time around. The body of work I had amassed in soft skills support became a valuable asset; this experience not only helped me create fresh training materials for US West™, but it also equipped me with the ability to learn how to train others effectively, even when I was struggling. It was proof that I was capable and that was of high value to me.

A fortuitous turn of events occurred while I was on my way to work one morning. A radio announcement informed me of a scholarship opportunity offered by the University of Denver. I decided to apply despite the requirement to take an academic assessment to qualify for the scholarship. The prize? A $50,000 scholarship for a bachelor's degree. Stepping into the testing site alongside a collection of other women, I struggled with emotions that would carry through the entire test. My responses to its questions were a mix of guesses and attempts to piece together solutions. I completely avoided the scratch paper provided; I was unfamiliar with problem-solving and was unwilling to showcase or leave evidence of my lacking skills.

Weeks later, I received the life-altering call that I had indeed won the scholarship. I promptly registered for classes, hopeful for what college might offer this time around. Yet reality proved daunting as I again navigated the challenges of higher education. During this period, I crossed paths with Dr. Carol Zak-Dance, a professor whose influence created a turning point in my life. She astutely recognized my communication deficits and courageously urged (told, bullied…) me to consider changing my degree plan.

Despite wanting to reject her counsel, I was primed to accept assistance. Copying books for an entire semester my first time in college underscored to me my need and readiness for support, and I felt a deep sense of gratitude for being noticed. The price for this opportunity was my entire $50,000 scholarship plus an additional $256,000 (to learn and master a marketable skill), which would be invested in my re-education (to become literate)—a journey that was a direct result of my lack of a formal education. This pivotal decision would compel me to confront my challenges head-on, requiring me to speak, write, and read in every course I undertook, no matter the difficulty.

Every time I think about the disparities between those with and those without disabilities, debt is one of the top things that comes to mind. Many people will not have to pay for their initial college experience because they started with the foundation of literacy that they received from a K-12 education. If someone leaves high school without that formal education, the staggering cost of learning a skill, the stress associated with that learning, and the demands on their tenacity are very high prices to pay.

I've heard just about every perspective about vocational education, college education, and joining the workforce with a high school diploma or GED. I've heard the arguments about college debt and how it's a choice. My perspective is and will always be: before you judge what someone has had to do to build a life, step completely into their shoes and provide a solution that meets their specific needs… or shut up.

I had a high school diploma and was illiterate. I tried a vocation and could not pass the required exams due to my disabilities. Ultimately, I went to college and obtained four degrees in order to finally build a career. I write this book today because people like me need options, and the first option is having a strong formal education so they can make choices instead of being forced into a one-size-fits-all approach. I write this because not every student learns or thinks the same, has the same level of grit, or understands enough about how to navigate the world on their own. I finally did what I did with the support of others who actually saw me and reached out.

Within poverty, there are often no parents who can take out loans on behalf of their children, and there are no jobs that pay enough to re-educate individuals who did not obtain a strong education initially without increasing their debt.

Many students are told to choose between learning a skill and poverty. My job at US West™ offered to train me in business or IT. Had I opted to apply their offered benefit of tuition reimbursement toward a business major, I would not have survived those classes. I understand that better now than I did back then. Oh, I knew I would struggle, but I didn't think I had any other choice but to try.

The scholarship was a possible jumping-off point, but I want to make something clear. An impoverished student without disabilities could use that same scholarship to get a degree and jump into their life and career if nothing else got in the way. An individual like me, with disabilities and literacy struggles, needed additional support to complete a degree, find a career, and build a life around it. That's not a statement that should bring pity, it's a statement that should bring perspective.

Speaking isn't just a skill; it's a gateway to learning, connecting, and expressing oneself. When a teacher poses a question, a classroom comes alive with a symphony of curious voices. Students raise their hands, hoping to contribute their thoughts to the ongoing discussion. Some voices are confident and clear, while others are a bit shy, tiptoeing into the conversation. But each voice is a brushstroke on the canvas of shared learning.

My experience with speaking was challenged by my disabilities. I had to watch, rewatch, listen, and practice in private before finally speaking in front of others. It wasn't just speaking the sounds of words that was hard; it was also difficult for me to form some sounds. I formulated words in my head, but my mouth didn't always say them correctly, or I thought I had the right words, but I didn't. I pronounced the combination "stra" as "scraw." I sometimes stutter, and speaking the wrong words in the wrong group of people might mean ridicule. Ridicule was memorable and taught me that I could never live down a mistake. If environments were noisy or voices were muffled, conversations (especially nuanced ones) were more challenging for me to understand. I also spoke in whispers when I was sick or drained.

Speaking incorrectly steals the winds of the heart's sail. Speech was the first place I learned to mask because if I could use my tone, body language, or street savvy to pretend I was the same as others, it was easier to fit in. The best way that I can describe this type of speaking is masked speaking - mimicking how others speak to one another to hide in the crowd. Learning to speak the language of each classroom meant I could safely engage in course content dialogues without the stigma associated with flawed communication. I have since learned that if I don't speak it, I avoid it, and if I avoid it, I do not learn it.

While I had learned the skill of writing symbols that enabled me to physically transcribe language, writing to communicate involved a deeper and more intricate process of organizing thoughts, expressing ideas effectively, and engaging readers. It is a dynamic blend of creativity, language proficiency, and rhetorical finesse that empowers writers to convey their message with impact and resonance. By simply putting the symbols of letters and language together, I could pretend to understand the elements of reading and writing when I did not.

Not all children with disabilities mask this way or get stuck in this part of the process. It is essential to identify that this process is not simply about the symbols of the alphabet. It is about the symbol of words, sentences, paragraphs, and larger bodies of information. People presume that once you appear to identify a single symbol, you are a reader. Yet, I had to write those symbols multiple times before I could identify, retain, and read them. The shape of a letter is only sometimes unique in my head because so many words start with the same letter. As a person with dyslexia, identifying a letter visually is not always accurate for me; my eyes and brain play interesting tricks.

For me, writing tends to happen in a mindless vacuum but I have to physically put letters on a page to have them make sense.

Once I write what I see, it takes a conscious act to begin to read what I write. It then takes another conscious act to retain it. Additionally, once one symbol was placed with another symbol, such as putting the letter "a" and the letter "t" together, it became an entirely different symbol. The same is true of a sentence or paragraph. Each new combination created a new symbol. This required me to discipline myself to practice writing things that were said in class multiple times. I would then practice reading what I had written. I'd go back and write my text books and then read them after I had written things out.

After years and years of copying textbooks so I could respond to questions in classes and still not retaining information, I made a huge discovery while working through my doctoral degree where I was failing again. Unlike my bachelor's and master's programs, there was too much information to copy. I could not retain it. I began to really have a hard time engaging in classroom content during my classes. Because the degree cost so much, I feared that I was putting my family in a horrible position. The stress of that began to cause a decline in my spirits. I decided to relieve stress by trying to paint.

I grabbed a few supplies from a hobby store and tried to Bob Ross my way to relaxation. Though I failed to "Ross" effectively, I did suddenly remember the information from my classes. I ran to my computer and started writing—really diving into the content like never before. I had to read it several times, but I kept painting between writing sessions, and it was the first time in all my life that the content was clear. It took me years to discover that I needed to paint to trigger my natural ability to write and communicate.

Learning to write in this way before focusing on reading established a solid foundation for understanding the symbolic nature of written words, building phonemic awareness, honing cognitive flexibility, and nurturing a deep engagement with the written word.

Someone might say I am a kinesthetic learner, but I leave that to the other researchers to figure out. Figuring out the role that painting could play in helping me to write was a major breakthrough.

Reading, though, has remained more challenging. Generally, I can learn in the short term by watching, but when I no longer see a demonstration, I forget the steps, and the same goes for many words when I am reading. I can read them for a while, but when I see them after a long break, I have to learn them all over again. If I'm not constantly in the content, I must build structures to bring information back.

Reading to comprehend remains an elusive skill, even after two master's degrees and doctoral work. I'm not ashamed; I'm just honest. Step-by-step written instructions are often impossible, as I tend to forget what I read and have to go back over the steps again and again, or I have someone read them with me. As a young person, I sometimes found this stifling. I can't tell you how many times I have heard the question, "Did you read the instructions?"

I read instructions repeatedly, and they still make little sense. Repetition of the task is not mastery, even when it seems like it makes sense to do it. Painting triggered something inside of me that built on the symbols and connected the symbols to the readings. I was even able to speak about concepts and found my passion was more alive the more I painted, wrote, and read. It was a stepping stone that would prepare me for my next great adventure - being a mom.

IV

PARENTING
(PART 1)

"You turned my lament into dancing;
you removed my sackcloth
and clothed me with joy."
Psalm 30: 11 (NIV)

On September 23, 1995, my life was forever transformed when I first held my newborn daughter in my arms. The journey to that moment had spanned over forty weeks of anticipation, marked by labor that stretched across five challenging days. An additional six days in the hospital followed, leaving me in a state of profound exhaustion. However, the fatigue was quickly overshadowed by the overwhelming rush of emotions that came with cradling my brand new baby girl. Uncertainty mingled with determination as I realized that I was responsible for her well-being and growth.

Beautiful, her skin was kissed by honeyed brown, her hair reminiscent of a starlit night sky, and her eyes an enchanting blend of caramel, walnut, and hickory. As the days turned into weeks, it became clear that her journey would not be without obstacles. Her initial struggles to breathe were followed by challenges with her skin. It took three arduous years of battling with medical professionals before we finally received a diagnosis of asthma and allergies. By then, her once-glowing skin had transformed into a pale and scaly exterior, and her eyes carried shadows of weariness. Her spirit remained unyielding despite it all; she was a beacon of internal resilience.

When the prospect of preschool came into the picture, I was filled with determination to provide opportunities to her that I had never experienced. I set up a miniature plastic table adorned with blue legs and yellow chairs, creating a space for early learning. A teacher's store nearby offered the familiar paper and number two pencils, reminiscent of my own school days. My daughter, typically compliant and adaptable, seemed like she would be eager to learn.

The excitement I felt was palpable as I carefully placed the letter "A" on the paper, an introduction to the world of letters. But her reaction caught me off guard; a subtle change in her expression signaled the shift in her countenance. Her eyes, a window to her emotions, seemed hurt, almost as if I had betrayed her trust. And her response was fiery—marked by angry words. She hurled a pencil.

I couldn't believe my eyes. This was not who she was.

This was not my kid.

We engaged in a battle of wills; though our age disparity was clear, the emotional dynamics felt complex, and the physicality left us both reeling. In the midst of the chaos, I recognized the need for a strategic approach to teaching my daughter. This marked the beginning of a new chapter, one that required innovative thinking and relentless commitment to a series of restarts that would pave the way for her growth and empowerment and my development as an educator.

Crafting a strategy for uncharted terrain requires meticulous research and thoughtful planning. My initial experience with reading felt like trying to hold sand in an open palm—details slipped through my grasp. With age, my ability to retain information gradually improved, but I still noticed that when new knowledge entered, older information often made its exit. I wanted my child to have a different experience.

My quest for a viable solution led me to explore rote memorization programs, however, the cost associated with these programs exceeded my financial means. Returning to my trusted companions—pencil and paper—I devised an alternative approach. I created index cards by folding and cutting sheets of paper into six equal squares, and I allocated a single letter of the alphabet to each square. Together, my daughter and I practiced articulating the letter's name aloud and presenting the letter visually.

With unwavering dedication, we followed this routine from Monday to Friday for a week, dedicating five minutes each day. To ease her transition into learning, I abstained from introducing writing at this stage, sensing a certain resistance from my daughter.

The first Monday after we started surprised me. As I presented a letter, my daughter's inability to identify it caught me off guard. Doubting whether she was playing around, I repeated the letter's name, only to be met with her genuine surprise and a look of unfamiliarity. This encounter was disconcerting, yet my decision to proceed with my course of action remained firm, especially since I had set aside funds to purchase a product that I saw online that was supposed to help parents teach early reading skills.

Week by week, I adhered to the same routine with my daughter, ensuring a gradual approach devoid of undue pressure. However, each week yielded similar outcomes, raising my concern even more. When the opportunity to acquire the professional product finally arose, her outcomes remained the same, regardless of the progress her step-siblings, my partner's daughters, were making with the same flashcards—identifying letters and delving into sound exercises. Evaluating a sample of her writing during this time, I realized she was still putting information, including her name, in the wrong order. I began having her tell me stories so that

I could write them down and read them to her, hoping she would remember them.

One of the stories she crafted was called *Elephant Tricks*. She had to put her name and a picture of the story on the front cover. On the top of the page, she put her name from left to right, she wrote "hariAh-M." Her name is Ah-Mirah. In the center of the page, she drew an elephant. A typical first-grade student would have drawn a two-dimensional character. My daughter created a three-dimensional elephant with no trunk and a thick tail. She did not recognize that she had written her name incorrectly. It appears that she started on the right side of the page and wrote "iAh-M" and on the left side, she wrote "har." The letters were out of order, but she had managed to put them in a quasi-straight line.

An image that captures how my daughter wrote her name

I recognized the need to prevent my daughter from falling significantly behind her peers and new siblings, and I knew it was time to pivot to Plan B.

Preschool was quickly approaching, and while she had a grasp on colors and could count to ten in a rote manner, identifying letters of the alphabet eluded Ah-Mirah. Ironically, she'd often sing the alphabet song, yet for her, the connection between the words in the song and letters on a page remained elusive. Adding to the challenge, though I had saved up money to invest in a professional educational product, the product received a unanimous chorus of displeasure from the children. They met the music and the voice of the speaker in the audio tapes with disdain. Despite weeks of dedicated effort, none of the children showed any significant progress in their learning. It was discouraging.

Moreover, the realization that my daughter would soon need to start writing added to my sense of urgency. I found myself stepping once more into uncharted territory. This time, we adopted a new approach with more steps than before. We practiced like this:

- Step 1: I audibly pronounced the letter.
- Step 2: I visually displayed the letter.
- Step 3: I repeated the letter's name.
- Step 4: I demonstrated writing the letter in front of her while articulating its name.
- Step 5: I assisted her hand in forming the letter while providing verbal guidance.
- Step 6: I prompted her to vocally echo the letter back to me.

Our time commitment increased from five minutes per day to fifteen or twenty minutes daily, Monday through Friday, as we integrated these additional steps. She made some progress, albeit not as much as I had initially anticipated. While my partner's children were progressing to confidently writing their names with neat penmanship, identifying keywords, and demonstrating some level of phonemic awareness, my daughter's advancement was slower. By the end of a week, she could identify the alphabet and recall some letter names, but by the start of the next week, much of what she had gained appeared to slip away. The process of writing letters independently remained a challenge, necessitating a painstaking, step-by-step approach.

As she entered school, her handwriting was so bad that her name took the form of large, sprawling circles across her paper. While she could verbally communicate her name, she struggled when asked to identify individual letters consistently. We continued the same step-by-step strategy as she progressed through her early school years, though her progress was limited.

By second grade, concerned calls from her teacher and principal began to mount. School staff meted out punishments to her due to her perceived slowness— her struggles to write her name and her inability to contribute to class discussions. She found herself excluded from outside activities or relegated to solitary moments while her peers got to enjoy time on the playground. I received calls from the principal's office that my daughter was being required to remain with him during recess, not for disciplinary reasons, but due to her perceived lack of pace compared to her peers.

This narrative felt all too familiar to me, harkening back to my own experiences, but this time I was the parent. Though our circumstances differed, the educational system's approach remained strikingly similar.

The outcome: Isolation.

While I moved my daughter to a new school, I still had to find ways to connect her learning to our work at home. I was attending school full time at night at the University of Denver, and working a full time job during the day. It wa going to be a challenge, but we needed to do something. My daughter was tested for an individualized educational plan (IEP), and though I had vehemently shared with the new school our lack of success with rote memorization tools in the past, the school was adamant that since we were out of the district, the only tool they were set to offer was a rote memorization tool. I'd even taken my daughter to our local Children's Hospital for an academic diagnosis. There she was diagnosed with ADHD, dyslexia, an auditory processing disorder, sensory disorder, and executive function disabilities.

The school identified her with Specific Learning Disabilities and Other Health Impairment. When I asked to have the doctor's diagnosis placed in her documentation, the school refused and noted that they identified everything except the sensory issues (though they had different titles on the IEP). Noting her disabilities did not sway their approach to educating her. For that school, my history as a parent, the doctor's diagnosis, and my daughter's struggles were not as important as what it would cost the teacher in time and energy to support my daughter in class.

I admit that I was angry and unsure of what to do next; I decided to take a day off and visit her at school.

I watched her come in and out of class, and each room required a different set of vocabulary or subjects that she needed to know, in addition to the vocabulary she was learning in her special education class. I called my boss and requested another day off. That day, I wrote down every vocabulary word or concept that she needed to know to be ready for school that week. She had ten or more vocabulary words per subject; she needed to remember discussions about each topic the day after it was reviewed; and she had to move quickly so that the other students would not have to wait for her.

Upon returning home, I carefully reviewed her diagnosis sheet and her IEP. Recognizing that the school's assistance was inadequate, I realized that my daughter needed a different approach—one that was now my responsibility to create. I had to either find a solution or equip myself with the knowledge to understand the situation better so that I could become part of the solution. The rise of internet resources enabled me to access valuable information and conduct in-depth research on a variety of topics— online books, math instructions, you name it.

The path to effectively teach my daughter was rife with challenges, often resulting in sleepless nights. Beyond the surface level of knowing her disabilities' names and their descriptions on paper, I had to comprehend the nuances and distinctions among these disabilities, particularly how they were manifesting in my daughter's experience. It feels simple when I lay it out on paper now, but it wasn't then. My daughter needed consistent support. My husband, my stepdaughters, and our two new young sons needed attention, too.

I was spending a vast amount of time then in hospital settings. In addition to her learning disabilities, my daughter had a chronic illness, and one of our sons was showing signs he might have it as well. Ah-Mirah had thirteen medications, and there were a lot of things I felt I didn't quite understand, but if I shuffled my priorities, I could find time in the day. That was the first thing I had to find. My resolve remained unshaken. For both her sake and mine, I needed to persevere.

So I did.

I put the kids and myself on a schedule, and I began digging through her diagnosis. The IEP only identified two categories of concern, but they were right in that the categories connected to what the hospital had told me. The major difference was that the hospital gave me specific names, while the school used broader language. As stated previously, my daughter's diagnoses from the hospital were ADHD, dyslexia, an auditory processing disorder (APD), sensory disabilities, and an executive function disorder.

These conditions showed up in a variety of ways. My daughter engaged in perpetual movement—she was a chair rocker and a non-stop conversationalist (except when it came to the classroom). It's not just a mother's observation; it's something that consistently appeared in her teachers' reports. She adopted a quiet and respectful demeanor inside the classroom, yet her struggle to remain physically still was evident. This occasionally led to unexpected movements like slipping off her chair during a quiet moment. While she would promptly apologize, it wasn't long before the pattern repeated itself, and she wound up in the principal's office.

Given the chance to be outdoors—though this was infrequent due to her severe allergies—she thrived in constant motion. Whether she was navigating the blacktop, humming melodies to herself, or engaging in conversations with anyone who would lend an ear, her energy and chatter were ceaseless.

At the other end of things, though, she struggled to arrange letters and words in sequence. Her ability to link letter symbols was disrupted. When she faced tasks requiring her to make these connections, she exhibited challenging behaviors (particularly at home by either shutting down, distracting her siblings, or talking back), withdrew, or completed the tasks slowly and with a sense of difficulty (both at home and in school). As a result, she started doubting her abilities and began viewing herself as unintelligent, perceiving a contrast between her and her peers.

She had difficulty with more than two commands or instructions at a time. She couldn't keep them in her mind. I saw this during her exam at the hospital. She was asked to run down a long, narrow hallway, touch the nose of a clown five times, and run back. My daughter ran down the hall, touched the clown's nose, ran back, and proceeded to complete that task five more times.

As I watched her tiny little legs stampede up and down the hallway, I caught a glimpse in my memory of the first time we sat down to write. From that moment in the hospital hallway, I realized that writing the letter "A" had more than two steps and that Ah-Mirah would have never been able to articulate to me that she didn't understand how to hold the three steps of writing the letter. I then recalled how many times I'd had to remind my daughter of a task. How often I got upset with her when she didn't respond or could not recall a task or list.

I'd be lying if I didn't acknowledge the shame that overwhelmed me at that moment.

Through my personal experience, side readings and research, I came to understand more about her sensory processing disorder. She sometimes had a visceral reaction when things touched her, and processing sensations in her body was different for her than others. This went beyond her eczema. When she had surgery to remove her tonsils, she expressed that she had pain in her tongue. When hit by a car, she could not say where she felt pain. If she was blindfolded and you tapped her on the arm, she would not be able to identify the location of that tap. She thought flowers were stinky. Many fabrics bothered her. Food textures, like eggs, were a problem. Most environments were uncomfortable for her; she struggled or had some kind of medical symptom (even with no evidence of a medical issue).

She struggled with organization, time management, self-regulation, and working memory, but she did the best she could. Of course, I struggled with these things, too. The intense research I underwent to educate myself so I could help her had to begin with me addressing my lifelong struggles and facing the masks I had created to mask myself. I could no longer pretend to be organized and look polished; I had to *be* organized because I was going to be the planner.

Incorporating a behavioral plan was essential because her behaviors at the beginning of our efforts were not conducive to her school performance or long-term success. Addressing these behaviors was critical to ensure she could thrive academically and eventually sustain a job. And given everything I had learned personally about the importance of literacy, at the smallest level, I needed to find ways to connect symbols to letters or words and improve her writing speed. Each step had to be clear and concise, utilizing basic instructions. I knew my pencils, papers, and pens were about to experience significant usage. To ensure balance, I limited her outdoor time so we could focus on these crucial indoor activities for her, and I created outdoor options for the other children so that everyone's needs got met.

My daughter—mighty and strong!

For the most part, although it was somewhat complex and time-consuming, our work together was showing promise. I observed progress in my daughter at home, although her progress in school remained slow. The multitude of vocabulary words across various subjects prompted us to transition back to using index cards. On one side of the card, she would write the word, and on the other, she'd put down its definition. This extra step appeared to be beneficial. My daughter embraced this approach, managing to retain vocabulary—at least for the week—enough time to perform adequately in some tests by Friday, just like I had.

I initiated the practice of having the kids recite stories to me. After I typed them into the computer and printed them, the kids illustrated their stories in newly created books. We would bind them using staples or repurposed notebooks. Occasionally, I'd read their stories to them at night. Yet, both the kids and I were bathed in weariness. I struggled to find time to grasp each child's progress in school. The situation was compounded when I learned that my eldest son also had a form of learning disability. Strategies that proved effective for my daughter didn't yield the same results for my son.

While my stepdaughters resisted the structured routine, their reading skills continued to develop. Trips to the museum and zoo, even when abbreviated, offered enjoyable experiences for them. Our days featuring home movies and indoor recesses brought joy to me. We didn't need to have much to make it fun; a few sheets and a flashlight make a great camping experience.

Still, my eldest son presented a unique challenge for me as a parent as I tried to help him learn. Our personalities often clashed, creating a mismatched teacher-student dynamic. He displayed an eagerness to absorb information, articulate thoughts, and even commit words to paper. However, his behavior leaned toward being argumentative, frequently challenging authority figures. Moreover, his distractibility could be excruciating—except when he was engrossed in the History Channel™. Knowing this, I gave him extended hours in front of the television, driven not by a desire for him to understand history, but because I was in pursuit of content that would captivate his interests. In my childhood, I used television as a coping mechanism and a way to understand people so I could blend in. Now, I needed access to information that would help my son connect to his education. He needed to visually see information when he was unable to read it in a text. Looking for videos and shows about history was an accommodation to help him master content while he worked on his reading skills.

As a student, he perplexed me. While he seemed to grasp the work we did on specific subjects, he struggled with reading a book. It was as if he was decoding a foreign language. He'd engage in imaginative play, often losing track of his surroundings. As I've said, his distractibility was prominent, even during activities he enjoyed. Providing instructions and monitoring his progress became a constant task for me. The challenges I faced with my daughter paled in comparison to those I faced with my son. I had to return to square one.

V

HIDDEN GEMS
(PARENTING PART 2)

"I am certain that I will see the LORD's goodness
in the land of the living.
Wait for the LORD;
be strong, and let your heart be courageous.
Wait for the LORD."
Psalm 27:13-14 (CSB)

Our family embarked on a research journey that started with me and evolved throughout the lives of my children, although I didn't realize in the beginning that we were on a research journey. I wasn't a scientist; I was a mom. Each wall we hit in an academic and personal setting forced us to recalibrate.

My oldest son Alex's experience with education is the reason I finally cracked the code on learning and teaching. When Alex was eight years old, he went through a deeply traumatic experience. An educator at his school dismissed him entirely. This educator conveyed to our family that we should accept our son's inability to learn based on the fact that her daughter faced similar challenges and never progressed. That statement wasn't just harmful, it set me off. I was ready to prove to her that she was wrong about my son and about her own daughter. I was very upset; that comment diminished his faith in himself and he is still working through it in many ways. To make matters worse, this educator, while speaking to another teacher within earshot of our son, called him "stupid."

My son spoke slowly, not incorrectly or incoherently, but at his own pace, and he was not stupid. This incident had a profound and damaging impact on my son. He was already grappling with numerous school-related issues, and at the age of eight, this experience hit him like a punch to the face. I had no way to soothe his emotional pain.

He often got distracted, engaged in conversation in class, daydreamed, wandered the room, and stalled. While he knew the letters and their sounds, he couldn't read without feeling drowsy. Whether he was speaking to someone or reading aloud, it took a considerable amount of time for him to articulate a sentence.

One day, his classroom teacher invited me to participate in a small group reading session with her and my son. As my son began reading aloud, what he read seemed like gibberish. The teacher and I exchanged perplexed glances before asking my son, "What did you just read?"

My son gazed down at the book, placed his finger at the end of the sentence, and started reading backward across the page. After a few moments, he looked up, surprised, and said, "Oh, I did that wrong."

He then restarted from the beginning of the sentence. Despite his efforts, he struggled to read through that short book. Whenever he began reading in the wrong direction, we could see him take a deep breath before trying again. As he yawned, tears welled up in his eyes, and he nearly fell asleep. A revelation struck me like a light turning on. No wonder he fell asleep everywhere—he was exhausted. Recognizing the urgency, his second-grade teacher suggested an IEP evaluation, and we started formulating a strategy to assist my son. My son slept as soon as we got home, and I could understand why.

However, the school's support was limited. The special educator, who boasted over twenty years of experience, resisted our requests for additional resources. She grew angry when we pursued an IEP. She even accused my son of feigning his learning difficulties due to our discussions about dyslexia. Considering the complexity, it would have been quite a stretch for an eight-year-old to orchestrate such a ruse. Just like it did with my daughter's situation, the school disregarded my older son's medical and psychological evaluations.

Alex is telling one of his amazing stories.

My son's evaluation meeting (for a possible IEP) was heavily impacted by my son's performance during the IQ test—the psychologist testing him had reported that my son raised his hand and declared he was finished in the middle of the IQ test. Then, Alex started falling asleep, and the evaluator couldn't reengage him to continue. The school believed that he should have completed the test to provide a more accurate measurement of his IQ. When we questioned why they didn't retest him at a more suitable time, they explained that he would have known how to respond if given another chance, skewing the results.

The psychologist said Alex "performed better on parts of the test than I could have, so he will remember the test, and the answers will not be spontaneous."

We countered that Alex didn't know the correct answers; he might only remember what he already answered. Despite the glaring discrepancy between the measured IQ and his actual school performance (a difference of over 29 points in some places), the school refused our request for an IEP.

They claimed that my son was making progress in class ever since we began working with him at home—the day we noticed him reading backward. According to the school's assessment, while my son was two grade levels behind his peers, he had the "potential" to improve, considering his progress in the forty-five days following our discovery of his reading issue.

When we explained that he was spending three to five hours per night on homework at home, they agreed that this was excessive and requested we limit it to twenty minutes. But when we attempted this adjustment, his performance plummeted. Even as his teacher highlighted this, the committee seemed indifferent.

The choice appeared to be between severely restricting his homework, thus, allowing him to fail with minimal to no improvement or keeping his homework and stress level the same—at a very high level—so that he could keep up with his peers.

Meanwhile, my son was forbidden from participating in science clubs or after-school academic activities because he wasn't "academically ready" for such challenges, according to the school (thankfully, his teacher ignored those requests). Clearly, he was penalized for having learning disabilities that were medically diagnosed but not officially acknowledged by the school.

The situation took a significant downturn when the school's special educator labeled my son as "stupid" within earshot of him. The trauma she caused him at that moment tested my instinct to solve the situation with my hands. While I couldn't resolve it by yelling at her either (that would only hurt my son more), I was infuriated.

I reached out to the principal and superintendent of the district. Their responses were to justify the conversation, noting it was a private talk between educators and that my son was eavesdropping. It was infuriating to see people justify their actions toward my son.

That very evening, after the stress and frustration of these events, my son had a remarkable dream. He described it to me as I sat in awe. He spoke of being an elf, living within a forest named the Dark Woods, which was situated within his thick, beautiful black hair. His dream involved a king and queen sphinx, ruling over a divided kingdom. The queen's domain was surrounded by clear water, symbolizing justice and truth. On the other side, the king's land was encircled by blood, representing the strictness and rigidity of the law. My son described his dream as a profound journey he took to mend the division between the two kingdoms.

This dream was too remarkable to ignore. I owed it to him to do something with it. I expressed my pride in him for sharing the dream, grabbed a pencil and paper, and documented his words. Over the weekend, we decided to turn the dream into a book. He chose characters, assigned names, developed their personalities and habitats, and determined the structure of the book—the number of chapters, pages in each chapter, and the level of detail manageable for him to read at once. This consideration was crucial, as overly thick books discouraged him. The process was incredibly enjoyable, and we weren't concerned about typos or rigid writing norms. Our focus was on capturing the essence of his narrative.

Unbeknownst to me, Alex had been secretly teaching his younger brother Anthony the phonetic codes that he himself was struggling with. One day, as I was reading quietly, Anthony, who was three years old, stood next to me and asked, "Mom, will that lady die?"

Perplexed, I asked, "What lady?"

"The lady in your book. She's in danger," he replied, concern etched on his face.

In response, I shut the book, turned on a movie, and requested that he read the words on the screen.

"Feature Presentation," he proudly proclaimed.

When I questioned him about how he learned to read, he attributed it to his older brother. He said his brother was teaching them when they were playing in their room. This was an unexpected twist, and it was the moment when peer teaching became the final piece of our process.

In our home, we plastered the story on the walls, drew characters, researched mythical creatures, and created intricate maps. When we completed our efforts, we had outlined all four chapters and written three of them. I printed the first book to give my oldest son something tangible, a book that he could hold and call his own—a book the school couldn't take away from him. This experience enabled him to see that he was not "stupid."

His pride soared, and before long, my son was an independent reader. His pace might have been slower than others, but he was undoubtedly a reader. From the challenges of navigating his unique learning style to the triumphs that emerged through innovative strategies, we've together witnessed the power of understanding, compassion, and adaptability. *The Dark Woods Series©, a* companion collection to this work, is a model of all the strategies in action.

I have always considered my children to be miracles. They have taught me more than I could e ever have imagined possible—from my first-born daughter to my new (to me) stepdaughters, to my first son, and finally to my last son. My youngest, however, taught me a lot about how important relationships and structure are to children. Like I did as a child, he showed us adults hints about his disabilities long before he was identified as autistic.

It was not just that he learned to read early. He clung to me. He had to be in or around my lap all the times, and it had to be on his terms. When he began to speak, he spoke fluently, even when his voice sounded like a toddler's voice. Most of our children made efforts to participate in small talk because they were socially curious. My youngest was not socially curious. He wanted nothing to do with other children unless they were family (and even then, he didn't seem to care to truly connect).

When I took him to daycare, he would cry until he vomited (projectile vomit - not just the slide-down-your-face stuff). I would have to turn the car around or wait in the parking lot until the people in the facility told me to come pick him up. He began using the word "stupid" to describe other children. He struggled with his teachers, and we could never use the word "good-bye" around him. That word sent him into a massive tantrum. We finally found a babysitter he would stay with. She refused to speak to him like he was a baby, and she was the only person he was calm with outside of family. To this day, he still struggles to spend time in groups, becoming overwhelmed and fleeing to his private spaces.

During his early years, we requested the help of a program in Colorado called Child Find. For the initial interview at the program's facility, parents leave their children with a group of other kids while they are interviewed in another room. I took my oldest son with me, and while he played with the other children, my youngest stayed in the corner and cried. He didn't look at the other children and if they came near him, he was rude. He was never rude until he was around other non-sibling children, and that was not how we raised him.

Eventually, the staff at Child Find called us back to complete the remainder of the evaluation. The evaluator began to speak to him, and she used a tone that adults believe is appropriate with children. Immediately, my son responded by mocking the way she spoke. Using a demeaning tone, he restated every question to the evaluator as if he were speaking to a child. It was the first time I had seen him mock an adult. I was embarrassed, apologetic, and curious all at the same time. When asked to stack blocks, he built them with ease and then glared at the evaluator.

At one point, she looked at me and said, "Intelligence is not your son's problem."

She then dismissed us and refused him services. She never told us what was going on.

Following that visit, I started taking notes about what we were seeing in our youngest son. He appeared to be more concerned about saving insects and connecting with pets than he was about connecting with peers. He only needed to watch something once before he could explain it in specific detail. When he started preschool, he could repeat all of what the teacher said, but he would not sit in a whole group with other children. Once he understood a concept, he was not willing to do homework.

He needed to touch on his terms, and he was highly specific about his routine. This was apparent whenever I would take the children to the museum and the zoo. My son had a pattern that we had to follow for every visit. The routine at the museum was two hours with dinosaurs, a snack break outside of the museum, two hours in the physical science section (how the human body works), lunch outside, one hour in the science exhibit (space), snacks outside, thirty minutes looking at rocks, and then a quick tour of the taxidermy animals. During visits to the zoo, we had to go left on some days and right on others, depending on his whim. It was a process.

My son was specific about who he would listen to (most often: his siblings), and he had many talents, including photography, football, robotics, cooking, and working with animals. When he was eight, he won honorable mention in an art contest for adults for a photo he took of his brother.

My youngest son received an "honorable mention" award at an adult art show.

With all his talent and his advanced reading level, it became difficult to help Anthony identify an internal motivator that would encourage him to comply with specific external requests, like those of his teachers. His logic was that he didn't have to prove what he could do if he knew he could do it. We tried to find projects that would connect him to a sibling while simultaneously helping us to see that he really did understand the work.

One of my favorite projects our family worked on was the redesign of our dinner table into a large board game. I took a cheap but sturdy table and we created rules and made a board game out of it. Each of our children had to learn a foreign language for school—our oldest chose Chinese and our youngest, Anthony, chose French—so we integrated language questions in the game.

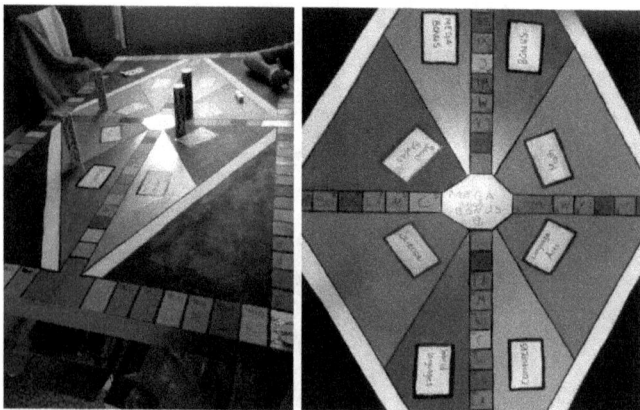

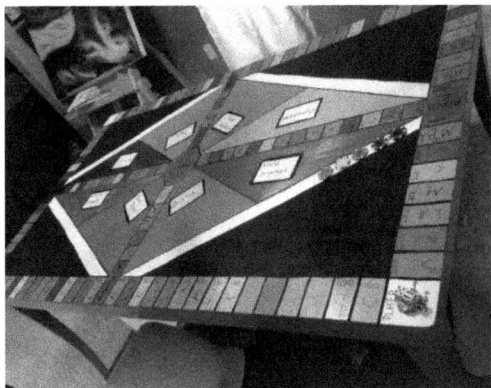

Topic: Chinese
Q: What does (名字)
Míngzì mean?
A: name (general)

Photos of the playing boards we created on our table and one of the game cards for foreign languages.

The project helped the boys to connect, and it challenged them to come up with more facts than their siblings, but it was harder to keep our youngest interested long-term. For that reason, I had to look a little deeper at our strategies. My youngest was eventually diagnosed with autism spectrum disorder (ASD), and I had to learn to address his behaviors and how they related to academics. As is evident, this was the third time I was invited to dive into new information to help one of my children learn successfully. I tend to always shove things over to prioritize and hyperfocus on the most important thing, and my children's ability to learn was always the most important thing. I kept adapting plans and they kept falling short of my expectations, so I found myself repeatedly starting anew. While I grappled with discouragement, there were instances when the allure of giving up beckoned me—a tempting escape from my struggle

During these times of uncertainty, I sought solace in prayer, seeking the inner resolve I needed to press on. I reflected on my own educational journey, which was tainted by shame and stigma, and I considered the legacy I wished to shape for my children. The terrible thought of them later discovering that I didn't do enough for them stirred a determination within me—an impetus to take action despite any lingering doubts.

After I completed my doctoral degree, I decided to pursue teaching in a public school environment. To my surprise, this path required obtaining another master's degree in curriculum and instruction. The master's program involved taking a full-time teaching position during the day and attending night and weekend classes for a small monthly stipend. Upon its completion, I would be licensed in general education (grades K-6), special education (grades K-12), and culturally and linguistically diverse education (English Language Learning, grades K-12).

While I was in this graduate program, I had the privilege of witnessing my daughter Ah-Mirah accomplish remarkable personal milestones. Over time, she transitioned from being academically three grades behind to successfully reaching grade-level standards by the fifth grade. When she entered her sixth-grade year, she was enrolled in advanced classes, and by high school, she was in a STEM (science, technology, engineering, and math) program. At the end of her tenth-grade year, she needed only seven more credits to graduate from high school.

At her school, however, the situation was in many ways untenable. One teacher called my daughter out during class for her disabilities and notified the whole class that the teacher would not accommodate her. Another threatened to fail Ah-Mirah in PE because she could not complete a test that required her to run outside after a severe allergic reaction. On top of these incidents, the school outright refused to allow her to graduate early, so we moved our daughter to another district.

To enroll as a senior, she was required to take four college-level courses during the summer, and she passed with straight As. She completed her final year in the top seven percent of her graduating class, though she was unable to walk at graduation or receive honors because she had not spent two years in the new district. Regardless, she went on to earn a bachelor's degree in three years' time. Subsequently, she completed three master's degrees in the fields of business and mental health.

Meanwhile, my eldest son Alex was preparing for standard classes and devoted his summer months to reading from an advanced reading list. And my youngest son Anthony, who was diagnosed with autism, exhibited advanced reading abilities of his own.

My children's and my challenges and successes formed the background I had entering the master's program, and while the program was comprehensive for general education students, it fell short of adequately supporting students who did not fit the conventional mold. I recall a particular incident that exemplifies my experience within this educational setting. One professor, who taught special education classes, was determined to help us understand the lived experience of individuals with autism, even though he himself was not autistic. He drew from his personal history of growing up with a deaf or hard-of-hearing brother. During one class session, he exposed us to sensory stimuli by activating a siren and subjecting us to strobe lights in a dark room. This experience not only triggered my own sensory issues but also epitomized the limited grasp that educators often have of individuals like me.

Unfortunately, the rest of the special education training classes were primarily based on perspectives from individuals outside of my disability community, people who had determined the level of support disabled learners needed based on theories from researchers rather than information from lived experiences. While research theories are valuable in categorizing different disability types, the curriculum designs that stem from them primarily focus on methods that are successful for students without disabilities and lack the necessary foundational support to build long-term skills for those who do have disabilities.

VI

TEACHING IN SPECIAL EDUCATION

"He comforts us in all our affliction, so that we may be able to comfort those who are in any kind of affliction, through the comfort we ourselves receive from God."
2 Corinthians 1:4 (CSB)

Entering a public school classroom in 2014, this time as an adult, student teacher, was strange. The smells in the hallways, the cafeteria food, the small people running around in groups, and realizing that I was responsible for my students' learning were consuming. I was excited and nervous.

In the building where I began my assistant teaching, special education was relegated to two tiny, closet-like spaces with just enough room for two desks and one table—one desk for each teacher (pushed into the far back corner of the classroom) and one kidney bean-shaped table for a small group of students, which left barely enough room to walk around when the room was full of people. There was not a lot of wall space for student work, so we had to rotate out examples between sessions. Filing cabinets for confidential student files lined a back corner, while workbooks were available on shelves. In front of the table, which held as many supplies (also called manipulatives) as we could stock In labeled storage bins on every shelf. Space was important for peer work, and while my students had to find space on the floor, students in Gen Ed could sit comfortably at their desks.

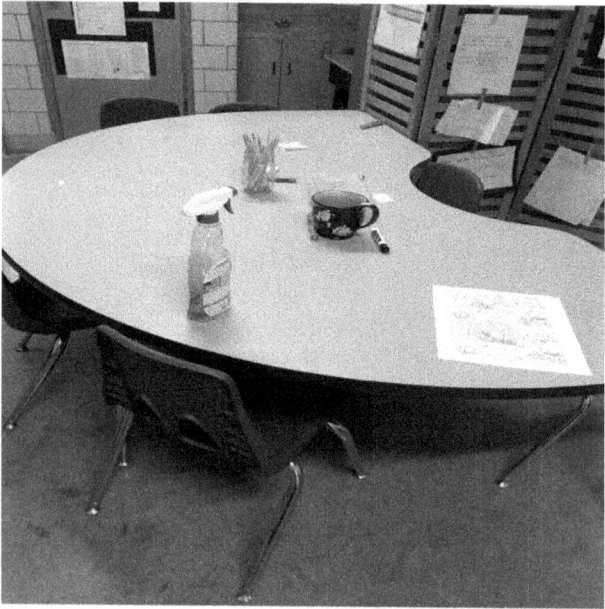

Small Special Education Classroom

My introduction to my new students was quick; my job was to sit and watch my designated mentor teacher for the first two weeks and learn the schedule, students, and lessons. My mentor spent the day doing phonemic awareness drills, adding and subtracting small numbers, and moving room to room to check in on students to make sure they understood the assigned work in their general classes. She had up to five students in each small group, but they ranged in age and ability levels based on the schedules of the general education teachers. No one group was created based on similar needs, which meant students in fourth grade were placed with students in first grade. Students who had difficulty sounding out words at grade level were placed with students who threw chairs or refused to open a book.

Our primary goal was to pull students out of class during the time that they had electives or for part of their literacy or math classes. A majority of the lessons we offered were focused on rote memory and were unconnected to the general education curriculum. The majority of reading posters were laid on top of one another. Regardless of their grade level, students practiced three- to five-letter words during our pull-out literacy class or numbers up to 120 (some under twenty) for addition and subtraction. We used analog clocks to teach time, reminded the students about months and days, studied the patterns in addition and subtraction, and counted change up to twenty-five cents. And though we ticked off items for literacy comprehension, we were primarily trying to get students to remember prior special education classes or to think about concepts that simply did not connect for them.

When I began teaching lessons, practicing exactly what I observed in my mentor, I saw limited to no progress with my new students, which was similar to what I observed when I started teaching my own children.

At some point during the year, my mentor teacher left the classroom, which put me at risk of having to move locations because I did not yet have the licensing to write IEPs on my own. Though I was not a fan of the curriculum, I did care about my students and wanted to see them through the year. To keep me from moving schools, the principal provided me with several fully licensed special education teachers to support me, though they were subbing in from retirement,

I spent about a week going from class to class, grade to grade, and reviewing what students were learning in their general education classrooms, and I revamped every lesson for my special education classroom. I replaced the special education vocabulary list with vocabulary from the general education classrooms. I purchased, borrowed, and collected donations of books at each grade level that connected to the content, and I looked for stories to connect math to real-world events.

Once I was able to take over the classroom, my new staff and I got creative. We did twelve sessions per day, a combination of pull-out and in-class lessons, and we held lessons inside and outside of the school building. I conferenced with teachers often and checked in on behavior and academic progress. For behavior modification, I continued before school breakfast breaks to help students remember strategies to help them during the day. We held lunch conversations to provide time with peers to debrief how the morning went and how the afternoon was shaping up, and we did small tours of the school to discuss appropriate behavior in each setting (classroom, lunchrooms, hallways, fire drills, gymnasiums, recess, main office, etc.). When creating a lesson plan, I considered every student I taught and reminded myself to build in strategies that wouldn't out the student's challenges but will become so commonplace that everyone in the class benefited from them over time. I still use this strategy.

I had to know that my students were able to contribute to discussions and participate in assignments more independently than they had before we started our new lessons. I started to see the kids develop, and so did the teachers. Focusing on literacy, I would write key phrases and vocabulary words from my students' general education classes on the board, the students would copy them, and then I would read them out loud to the kids as we worked through definitions and context. We pulled out sounds, worked through definitions, connected the terms to real-world events, and wrote sentences about them in our whole group sessions. Then, they would turn to one another and teach, in their own words, what they had learned.

By the end of the year, everyone had made progress. We were saving time because sessions began moving much faster as a result of the work we were all doing to adjust classroom behavior. The more students learned, the more they wanted to get started and teach others. This was where the rote memory techniques came back into play.

Students would use lessons from our classroom to do mini groups for their peers or for younger students. Peer-to-peer leadership was part of the teaching framework for the district, but with the work we were doing in special education, when my students went back to class, they were moving from being the ones taught in class to the ones teaching. The Gen Ed teachers noted that my students were connecting special education lessons to the classroom because the content was finally the same—we were just addressing it in different ways in the different classrooms.

Student behavior was concerning when I started. Some students had severe tantrums for so long that they were accustomed to setting off classrooms. We wanted to change that. One student in particular (let's call him Gus) was blowing up every day with his fifth-grade teacher. He was generally angry, but expressed joy in being able to frustrate that teacher.

Gus and I worked on strategies, and he would tell me, "Dr. Richmond, I know all of that, but she hates me, and she doesn't let me use my strategies."

One morning, I heard Gus yelling down the hall. To my surprise, he was in tears, screaming, "I'm not stupid, Dr. Richmond! I don't need that crap from her!"

I excused my pull-out group of students back to their classrooms, and I stepped with him into the hallway. He just melted to the floor. I'd not seen him this vulnerable before. I asked him to walk with me.

When I got Gus to stop crying, he told me how he just needed time to work out a math problem—he just needed a little time to think. This was a strategy we had worked on, him asking for more time, and his Gen Ed teacher had agreed to it. According to Gus, his teacher refused to wait. Instead of letting him figure the math problem out on his own and in his own time, she told him the answer.

"I knew the answer! I'm not stupid! Why can't she just let me do it? Now the class thinks I'm stupid too!"

Then I got it. In her attempt to move quickly, she broke our agreement and pushed him to move too fast. She didn't just break her word to me; she broke her agreement with the student. I'd spent months trying to find a compromise between this student and teacher in the formalization of a strong behavioral contract. When she pushed him in front of the class, the contract was ruined. He didn't even want to go back into the room.

This type of situation significantly impacts the lives of special education teachers and their students.

The day this teacher broke her agreement to our student, the school social worker was out, my special education staff was busy, and the situation took more than an hour for me to resolve, which forced me to reschedule all of my remaining groups. I was with Gus the rest of the afternoon, helping to reestablish trust and walking through strategies on how to accept things we can't always change. The next morning, I spent my breakfast group time working with him and had him back in class by the start of the first period.

The time I spent with Gus, because of something outside of his control, was a violation of all of my other students' right to education. The break in their time in my classroom and their routine impacts student learning.

As a result of this situation, I became firmer with other teachers during agreements for behavior contracts. I had to make sure teachers and parents understood what happens to students when promises are broken. Mid-year, the student whose contract was broken walked into my classroom in jeans with a suit jacket, white shirt, and tie. He proudly announced that he was going to have a great day and asked if he could spend time in the afternoon with me if he did. He did have a great day. More importantly, he knew he was going to control his day regardless of what other people did. It was progress. It became important for me to help students understand that who they are at one point in time is not who they will always be. They needed visuals they could point to. While I was there, the school changed its social studies curriculum to focus on the Civil Rights movement. I brought in an American history calendar, and the students and I mapped our history on that calendar on the back wall so we could tie our personal history into the history of the United

States. Each student brought in pictures and shared with the class their favorite family stories.

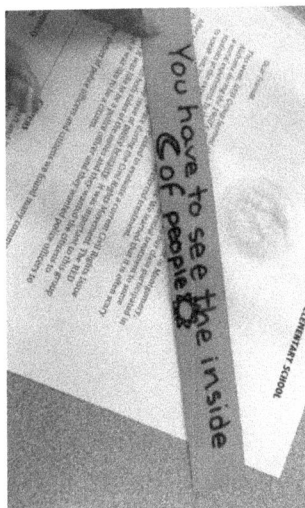

Civil Rights project

Family history lesson: Teacher/Student Timeline

We completed several author studies, had a gallery walk, and invited the staff to come and hear what the students had put together. One of our quietest students was in charge of providing pamphlets to people as they walked in. We plastered the walls with student work, and all twelve groups participated in decorating the classroom. As teachers entered, our quietest student blasted out, "Look what we did!" He then shared about the projects and what he had learned throughout the year. Prior to that day, people presumed that he was primarily non-verbal. His competence had been determined by his outward behavior, rather than his actual potential.

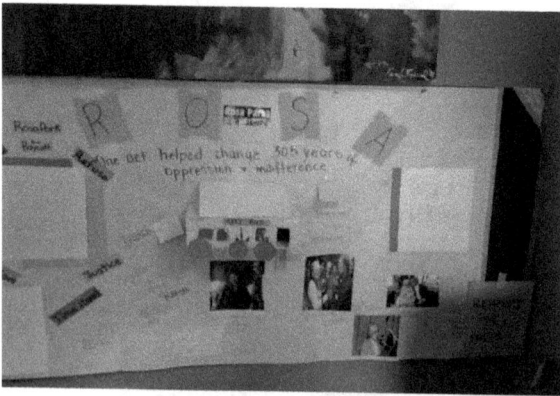

Rosa Park lesson:
Students created an interactive silent gallery walk:

My going away party.
All my students handmade gifts for me

At the end of that year, my students threw me a party. The school bought me cake, my students gave me hand-made gifts, and I received a video of advice from my students. The video was taken on my personal iPad while I was out of the classroom. It is, to this day, one of the sweetest violations of personal space I've ever had. The students also painted me my own personal tea set. I will forever be grateful for how each student shaped me that year.

Tagline: Tea set designed by my students

Over the course of this year, I had to do targeted research on multiple disabilities and cross reference academic and behavioral supports that were beneficial in mixed disability environments. I learned how to visualize lessons, to break down definitions and terms to build background on key terms. I found multiple books and videos on topics to help my students understand the content they were learning in the classroom. I took the phonemic awareness tools and revamped them to include words used in the state standards to help students understand what they should learn in every lesson I taught.

Having difficulty with language was a common thread between my students with disabilities and my students who were identified with disabilities who were learning English. This allowed me to use language proficiency tools (tools to help teachers understand when students who were from another country or who spoke another language were grasping content in English) as accommodations in my classroom. Putting in the hard work actually began to make my job as a teacher easier. I was able to create color coded spreadsheets that helped me to track my students and report growth. I'm not referring to how fast a student could read or write their facts on paper. My focus was on how they understood what they read, if they could tie it to a real-world situation/experience, if they could articulate what they knew, and if they could teach it to someone else. My students had as many ideas for projects as I did, and that made them feel like they had a voice. That is why my student teacher experience was so life-altering

Once I obtained my full license, I moved to teaching middle school at a Title 1 school in Aurora, Colorado Public Schools. I was assigned to teach students who qualified for moderate services (services that are provided to students outside of the general education classroom). These students were placed in two back-to-back literacy and/or math sessions each day, and because of their schedules, they could only attend one elective each semester. General education students received two electives each semester. That was concerning to me; though I understood that the district wanted to ensure students had the opportunity to develop, it still felt like a punishment.

This time, I had a classroom the same size as other general education teachers. I had room to put items on the walls. A majority of the classrooms in the building had no door and only a half wall on the side of the rooms connected to the hallway. This meant that my special education students had no privacy.

Middle school classroom

Students in the program were required to use scripted, research-based educational products for learning, which were selected by the district. It required students to use hand signals while sounding out simple sounds during a call-and-response section of the lessons. Anyone walking by would have clearly seen that lessons were not at grade level (as lessons sounded similar to what would happen in a kindergarten classroom), which would have exposed my students. I did not want that.

The content was also confusing, as the vocabulary from the start of the lessons did not prepare students for the actual reading sections later in the lessons. That bothered me a great deal.

Regardless, it was important to me to follow the program and make my lessons impactful without creating a hostile environment for my students with their peers. I removed the hand signals and call and response portion of the classes. I then looked for ways to connect the prescribed lessons to everyday life.

We found a way as we got closer to Christmas my first year at the school when a student in my class unexpectedly shared about the death of a parent. This occurred at the same time the class had to read a passage about constellations. After a discussion in the whole group about the loss of a parent, we decided each student in the class should write their own book about loss, using constellations as a backdrop to their stories. We found an online story editor, and we all wrote books. I then ordered two copies of every book, one for the student writer and one for me. We read our stories aloud in class.

From there, we used school-based magazines and student-based news stories to start our classes. We researched real-life people, and we even wrote letters to the President of the United States. At the time, the President stated that he wrote back to everyone who wrote to him. My students heard about it during one of the news stories we studied, and they asked if it was real. We only had one way to find out.

When the White House sent back a form letter to only one student, my whole class got excited to call the President out on his BS, and they wrote again. They received almost the same form letter again, which led the class to start creating more real news stories on their own. They interviewed teaching staff and looked for stories from their class content. They built weather stations in the classroom, and we had fun while we learned.

The following year, I had students who attended one general literacy class and one special education literacy class. I provided what the district called push-in class, meaning I would support my students in literacy and math classes in addition to providing services outside of the class. The concern was the same as the year before, as students frequently came to me and shared that they were lost in the general education classroom because they didn't understand the content; it was vastly different from the special education content. They felt they were not smart and that teachers did not care. They didn't understand, nor should they have been forced to consider, the fact that most general education teachers were not trained in special education, but most were doing their best to support the students they had.

My students had no idea of the combined effect of their academic and behavior realities on teachers in the classroom, but in my opinion, they were amazing people, and I wanted to give them something to hold on to. I needed to work harder to make my lessons count because many of my students were so far behind that their confidence was minuscule. For that reason, I went back to the drawing board and brought real-world examples with the same resources that I used with my children back into my classroom.

I found a way to connect each lesson to my life and encouraged the students to connect it to theirs. I purchased magazines, books, and math manipulatives, and I partnered with general education teachers. I started teaching grade-level math, social studies, and science concepts in my literacy classes. I added more English Language Learning support to my classroom, and I scoured the standards to highlight every time my students made academic growth. I encouraged my students, and they encouraged me.

I was watching my students develop, but I was stuck in a system that did not support ability diversity on a larger scale. The stress and time it took to develop lessons without access to grade-level content had me working from 5 a.m. until late in the evening. Though I wanted to stay, ultimately, I needed to change schools.

Moving to a K-8 school that allowed me to use my own tools provided me with a new type of freedom, though I still had to purchase my own supplies. Robbi and I estimated that I was spending around $350 each month for healthy classroom snacks. I had purchased some bulk supplies for about $1000 from the teacher store when the school year began each year. I can't remember how much I spent on manipulatives, because I made some of them. I should have kept track of supplies I purchased; It was a substantial amount. That is true of many, If not most, teachers. I participated in the general education setting and also provided pull-out services for students in this setting.

My groups ranged in age, but unlike my previous elementary school experience, I was able to create groups of students based on grade level. This helped me to build out my classes using grade-level work, which was a huge benefit to students. But there was still one myth that I was continually dispelling for curious teachers and parents who thought this would be a catch-all educational solution.

Connecting to grade-level content does not mean that any learner has retention of all concepts all the time. This is true of both students in general education and students who are in special education classes. The premise that students should not be able to move to the next grade level if they have not fully mastered the principles of the last grade-level concept they were taught has kept children with disabilities locked in programming since the Individuals with Disabilities Act (IDEA) was created. IDEA was modified in 1990, 1997, and then modified again in 2004. If a student hasn't achieved mastery, provide them with a tool to continue learning, and teach them how to use it.

The objective of learning systems should be to help students develop as many strategies as possible to live productive, independent lives. The more students have access to appropriate grade-level skills, the more they can adapt to challenges as they grow older. This does not always mean they achieve full mastery; it does mean students have a coping strategy when full mastery is not possible. We should not stop teaching children, and we should not give them the lowest level materials because that's easier on us in the moment. These approaches are not sufficient for children as they develop.

Students deserve to grow into adults who can know how to complete an application for a position and participate in work culture, even if they struggle to understand social behavior, and can understand the written word well enough to read instructions in a cookbook to prepare their own meals. They deserve to understand enough about geography to know how to read a map, give directions to their home to a visiting friend or relative, or put a pin in their location via a mobile app. They deserve to be able to use a calculator in the grocery store if they are unable to hold amounts in their head while shopping. Understanding these rights guided me as an educator in my new school.

The K-8 environment helped me to see more clearly when students' needs were misidentified, as those students would grow faster once they made real-life connections to the materials. When a student was misidentified and had access to real-life connections, they would move multiple grade levels in one year, whereas a student who should have been qualified moved one to one-and -a -half grade levels in a year on one or more standards when they had real-life examples. I learned a great deal about accommodations during this time as well.

Accommodations are supports that schools provide to assist students in class. Previously, my understanding was that teachers should provide as many accommodations as possible to students on IEPs, but my personal experience as an individual with disabilities, the experiences I had as a mom, and what I saw in my students told me a different story. The new story I was learning was that accommodations should be scaled back as children develop new skills. When children experienced some struggle, it built confidence, so this was important.

I began working with students, having them scale back their own accommodations. Our main goal each year was to prepare them to be independent by high school graduation. Independence doesn't mean that an individual has no accommodations, but that they understand employers are only required to provide reasonable accommodations, and that they know the difference between what employers may provide and what school provides.

If a student needed reading support at the beginning of the school year, near the end of the year, they would determine to what extent they still needed that support. This was only possible and confidence-building because there was no teasing about skills in my classroom (unless my students were teasing or correcting me). I praised my students when they caught me making mistakes, but the only person in my classroom outside of me who could correct a student was that student. My students had the most trouble in classrooms or with providers who stigmatized them based on their qualifications for the IEP. My students were often upset by teachers or providers who expected nothing of them or refused to support their basic needs. Teachers would frequently call out my students, accusing them of pretending, refusing accommodations, or in some cases, separating them from others in the classroom and not speaking to them.

I remember a beautiful young student I'll call Nick who had experienced terrible trauma. Nick's trauma impacted him so much that he was nearly nonverbal during his kindergarten year. When I met him, he could identify four letters and four numbers. His behavior was defiant, and his trust in adults was broken. It took some time for him to warm up to me. I captured some key concepts that I used to develop a plan for him:

Fortunately, Nick had a strong mind. We started slow. Short visits with an increase in expectations each time we met. In every session with him, we used grade-level work or work at the next grade level. He was called out of class often because teachers struggled to keep him under control in the classroom. Some had no idea how much Nick was growing; they only saw where he was starting from. He was, in all ways, a handful. However, reviewing his strengths and areas for growth monthly helped me to see when he was developing.

We ended his first-grade year with him knowing most of his site words, numbers to 200, and he was slowly developing as a reader. Still, his first-grade teacher made him sit by her desk without allowing him much access to the rest of the class to socialize. She remembered every mistake he made and used each as a reason to keep him from the main group.

His first-grade teacher kept his successes from the next teacher. The second-grade teacher created islands for all of her challenging behavior students and never knew which of them was even in the classroom. Meanwhile and against these odds, he was making huge progress. Outside of this, Nick had moved from first-grade content to second-grade content. His disruptive behaviors had dropped from several a day to a few per week. The second-grade teacher still did not acknowledge his success.

Nick knew his teacher didn't like him and often told me that he felt that she hated him. No second grader should feel that way. He still came to my class every day because it was a requirement, and because he knew I wanted to know he was in school. In my class, Nick taught an echolalic (a student who only repeats what they hear) autistic kindergarten student during our literacy session; a deaf and hard of hearing kindergarten student (someone with little to no functional hearing) during our math session; he supported three first grade students during our coaching sessions on behavior, and he was mentored by a student in the sixth grade who had affective needs (social, emotional, and behavioral problems).

The issue wasn't that he wasn't growing; it was that his reputation preceded him with Gen Ed teachers. His behaviors were so extreme when he was younger that by the time he made progress in the second grade, few general education teachers could see it. I firmly believe it was (and is) because many educators are not taught about the diversity of academic needs, and classrooms have so many disparate behavioral issues that teachers are struggling to address preventable behaviors in ever-growing groups of students when they're all in a single environment.

My memories of Nick are extensive, yet two stand out more than others. The first of these moments concerned his behavior. I spotted him one day on the way to class and asked him to walk with me. He complied and said, "I'm gonna end up in the detention room today." We had worked hard to keep him out of that room. It was not what you typically think of when you think of a detention classroom—it had computers, soft lighting, quiet corners, and no real requirement for academic work. My highest-behavior students acted up just to go there. Heck, I would have acted up to be in there too.

To motivate our students to be in and engage in their general education classes, I had created a room that my students hated being in. It was large, with no computers, no soft lighting, and one poster that read "I believe in you." We had one paraprofessional, one teacher, and a ton of academic work available for students who were kicked out of class. We did not make students stay in the room. When a student acted up in class, we would take them to the room to talk about strategies and get them reengaged with their school work. Students could be escorted back to class any time they wanted and were ready. Most of our students spent just one day in my space, and that was enough incentive to motivate them to stay in the classroom for the year. Unfortunately, the school did not like the plan, no matter how successful we had been, and took the space away. Since there was no other option but the other detention room for students, maladaptive, disruptive behaviors picked up with our population—immensely.

Nick and I had a plan on how to keep him out of detention, and it had been working well enough—at least his time up there was decreasing. So, when he told me he had plans to be in detention for the rest of the day, I dug in. "Why would you go there? We have a deal."

"I know, but I'm going to beat that kid up," he said matter-of-factly.

"Remember, there are other ways to deal with a student like that." I countered.

"Nope, I told the teacher. She told me to go back to my seat. He hit me again. I'm going to beat him up."

"How about you come to lunch with me instead?"

"If I see him first, I'm going to beat him up, and you can come eat with me in the detention room."

I looked at my phone to check attendance and noted that the student he was talking about had yet to sign in for the day. Feeling secure, I thought I would have time to finish my rounds and pick Nick up for lunch.

"I'll see you at lunch," I said as we met his teacher at the door.

A few hours later, on my way to his classroom, I saw him carrying his lunch tray.

"Where are you headed?" I probed.

"Back to detention. I told you I was gonna beat that kid up," he said proudly.

I huffed out a furtive breath and inquired why he was not with a teacher escort since he was in detention. He notified me I was his escort now.

You see, a child that smart who is only in the second grade is learning which behaviors are acceptable and unacceptable and to whom the rules apply. I felt he had no recourse but to defend himself because, for whatever reason, his teacher did not hear that he was being hurt. I'll remind you here that Nick was previously nonverbal due to the significant trauma he faced early in life. The trauma was not the teacher's fault, but it is one reason we have to train teachers better.

The second situation that comes to mind when I think of Nick was our work with a young, echolalic autistic student that I will call Cindy. Echolalic means that someone repeats what they hear, but they are not cognizant of what they are being asked. Nick and I would travel to the kinder room to pick up Cindy, and as we traveled down the hallway, we would engage her in the same conversation each day. We taught her when to say, "Good morning, Dr. Richmond." and "Good morning, Nick." She would do this, even in the afternoon, but she would at least address us.

We had been working on non-fiction texts, and Nick was excited to tell Cindy about a book called *Not Norman*[C]. We got to the classroom, and he wanted to be the one to hold the book. He did so proudly. I placed it right in front of her and asked her to tell us what she noticed in the picture on the cover of the book. After months had gone by without much of any acknowledgment about what we were saying, Cindy said, "I see me! I see Cindy!" Nick dropped the first tear. He screamed, "Yes! Yes, that is you!"

Looking at me, he just ran over and gave me a huge hug. Something was there, and he knew it. From that point on, he wanted to start every literacy class as the leader. When we moved to poems and read what we called *The Rain Poem*, whose real title I have forgotten, he was excited to help her create the sounds of the rain on paper. Once they listened to the sound of the rain on tape, they told me the phonetic sounds that they wanted to use. I had them rewrite my words on large pieces of paper, and we lined the hallway with our large paper rain poem.

Nick took Cindy to the start of the poem and hop-scotched his way through the hallway, holding her hand. When it was time to walk her back to class, he shared with her how proud of her he was, and she smiled, echoing his words.

When Nick finally left the school, not one teacher really understood his progress.

There are so many students like Nick and Cindy whom I think of today as I look back on my life in the public education setting. I spent just two more years in the public education system after working with them before I realized that my calling was to support teachers at another level, so that those teachers could have a greater impact on students.

VII

WEAVING IT TOGETHER

"Your eyes saw me when
I was formless:
all my days were written
in your book and planned
before a single one of them began."
Psalm 139:16 (HCSB)

When I was a child, some of my siblings and I would pretend to play school on the basement steps in our home in Park Hill. That basement was finished. It had the same floor plan as the upstairs, except there was a laundry room downstairs where the kitchen was upstairs. One of us would get up energetically and pretend to lead class or "Sunday school." The rest of us would sit on the stairs and watch. It was equivalent to watching a stage play. My uncle was my favorite to watch. His body movements and energetic voice would boom in the small stairwell.

When I was growing up, I never imagined that I would be a teacher in my adult life, yet I constantly found myself working with kids, either at a day camp, via babysitting, or through UpLift's mentorship program. As I grew up, I understood more about the development of children than I did adults. Children were typically honest about their emotions (good or bad), so you knew where you stood with them. Adults—not so much. Children needed to hear information twenty-one times, they needed touch to make connections, and they needed direction because they had to learn to think before they acted.

It's odd to reflect back and realize that I struggled to connect with most children when I was a child. I connect better with children now that I am an adult because I understand that children need certain support. The reverse is also true, that as a child I connected better with adults (or it appeared I did) and as an adult, I struggle to connect with adults because adults mask and hide their true motivations.

When I put all of the pieces together, I find that I was always on the path to become who I am at this moment.

Expressing my emotions was sometimes problematic, and that made forming friendships a deliberate process, as I preferred spending time alone to avoid social exhaustion. Engaging in social events wasn't my preference; I'd rather read or paint in solitude. Maintaining eye contact while speaking was a chore, and my direct communication style sometimes put people off. Although aware that I was missing social cues, I found it difficult to pinpoint exactly what

I was missing. Routines were my comfort, and disruptions tended to throw me off balance.

Self-awareness is the foundation upon which personal growth is built.

So, when I finally received the diagnosis of autism at the age of 40, I went back and apologized to my children for being rigid about rules and guidelines, especially about their exact words. I struggle with blurred lines, and a false statement has always been, to me, a lie. My children lived through my lack of understanding of my condition and its impact on them. They deserved for me to ask for their forgiveness, and I owe it to them to give them the time it may take for them to give it. I cannot teach them about self-awareness or self-acceptance if I can't be vulnerable with them. I have accepted who I am; I am working to be the best version of myself.

It was my daughter who ultimately helped me make the connection. As the children grew older, as I said earlier, they were required to take foreign language classes, and my daughter started a German class in high school. I was a bit shocked when she chose German, but I was thankful she was open to the challenge. I asked her, at some point, why she took to it more quickly than she took to the English language, and she informed me that it was like she learned her second language, English, first and her first language, German, second. I dwelled on that concept for a long time. It made me wonder if I struggled with English because it was not my first language.

So, when I was starting to fail in my doctoral classes, I went on a walk and found myself in an art store. As I also described above, I figured painting might relieve my stress. I picked up some supplies and went home to "relax." Not long after I picked up the paintbrush and started painting, I was able to remember what I had been learning. It was like the lights finally came on. I could not have told you what I was going to paint, but in the movement in my arm and the focus that I had while painting, once I stepped away from the canvas, I found the right filing cabinet in my head and the exact information that I needed to write my papers for class. In the span of a few years, I had painted over eighty paintings. I could finally speak, and it felt like home to speak through the canvas.

My challenges impacted my ability to communicate effectively, comprehend written and spoken content, and fully engage in academic and social interactions in an English-speaking environment. I needed help that ranged from basic linguistic tasks to higher-level skills like understanding context and making inferences. I was exhibiting the following signs:

1. **Listening:** I found it hard to filter out background noises and focus on relevant information. I often struggled to follow conversations or instructions in noisy environments. I could not remember definitions and terms or decipher non-verbal cues indicating shifts in conversations' meanings.

2. **Speaking:** My speech tended to be soft-spoken, making it difficult for others to hear me clearly. I

tended to communicate directly, which some people find off-putting. Maintaining eye contact while speaking was challenging for me. I struggled to comment on things in class because I was not certain I understood and could articulate information.

3. **Reading:** I faced difficulties with analog clocks and comprehending written content. Reading from computer screens was tough, and I needed extra time to process written information. Reversing letters and numbers contributed to my reading struggles, and my reading speed was slower than usual. Each new combination of letters was its own symbol and required effort to read with additional effort to understand the context.

4. **Writing:** Writing was a time-consuming task for me. I struggled to organize my thoughts and express them coherently in writing. Spelling and grammar errors were common due to letter and number reversals. My writing often required more effort and time. This resulted in many hours of practice in writing the symbols associated with language. I wrote what I didn't understand until I could write something that made sense to me.

5. **Oral Language:** My verbal communication was clear but lacked modulation. Because I tend to communicate directly, it sometimes hinders my social interactions and understanding of subtle cues. If exhausted, my responses became curt, and this came off as dismissive to others.

6. **Comprehension:** My comprehension abilities were impacted by reading and listening struggles. Extracting relevant information from written or spoken content required more effort from me. Comprehension became particularly tough with complex texts or in the presence of background noises that I was not familiar with.

Though I've explained some of the challenges I faced and my students and children faced, sometimes simply stating these things does not communicate their impact on an individual's life, nor does it outline how they might look to an educator. Educators are tasked to manage multiple behaviors at one time, while attempting to teach content (math, literacy, science, social studies,) and track behavior. When behavior spikes, it can be overwhelming. My empathy for my students comes from a place of understanding what it is like to have a disability. Teachers do not always have that history.

I want to share a useful analogy I call the Alphabet Soup Party that I created during my doctoral program. My committee chairperson asked me many times to explain learning disabilities. It's not that people don't understand the concept, it's that they struggle to understand how they impair people. I thought about it and asked her if she ever ate alphabet soup. She said she had, so I explained how to understand learning disabilities in this context.

Imagine a social gathering that revolves around sharing a meal. The host takes on the responsibility of providing the soup—a rich mixture of letters and words—evoking creativity and expressions of enjoyment on the faces of the diners. However, there's a catch: every attendee is required to bring their own bowl and spoon to partake in the culinary experience.

Now, most guests come well-prepared with their bowls and spoons, ready to savor the linguistic feast and engage in conversations. They effortlessly scoop up the letters, stringing them into coherent words and sentences, and engage in the delightful exchange of ideas. It's a harmonious scene where language flows seamlessly, connecting individuals and creating a shared understanding.

Now, apply this analogy to a classroom. The teacher brings the soup—the content. Most guests are typical learners, and the party is in the classroom. But for someone like me or many of my students, navigating the Alphabet Soup Party presents a unique set of challenges. Following are some possible ways that I or another person with disabilities might show up.

I could forget my bowl, so I'd find myself without the essential tool needed to capture and absorb the linguistic content. The words and sentences would slip through my fingers, leaving me disconnected from the conversation.

I could bring a plate instead of a bowl, which is entirely unsuited for the task at hand. I'd struggle to collect the letters and words effectively, resulting in a disjointed and unfulfilling experience.

I could forget my spoon. Though I'd have a way to contain the soup, I'd lack the means to fully engage with it and take it in. I'd struggle to gather the letters and words effectively, hindering my ability to participate.

I could also show up with a fork, knife, or ladle instead of a spoon. Sometimes, I might arrive with tools that are close but not quite right for the task at hand. These metaphorical utensils would hinder my ability to effectively grasp the language, leading to confusion and frustration.

In the middle of the soup party—or classroom—I could pick up my bowl and pour the soup on my head. There are instances where, despite having the necessary tools, I might struggle with coordination or understanding. Or my bowl could have a hole in the bottom, as when I possess the tools to engage in language but have gaps in comprehension or retention, which lead to an incomplete understanding of the conversation.

When the bowl and spoon don't align with my needs, at some soup parties, I might resort to using my hands—attempting to grasp and piece together the language in an unconventional manner. This makeshift approach can lead to miscommunication and misunderstanding.

And even if I have all of the correct tools for the party, I could hate the soup or be allergic to it. The classroom setting itself might be difficult for me to navigate due to reasons outside of my control. There's an assumption in education that we all learn the same way, in the same environment. We fail to see that the environment itself—lighting, loud sounds, and tones of voice—can keep students from connecting to the curriculum or teacher.

This Alphabet Soup Party analogy underscores the importance of providing the right tools and understanding to students to ensure a meaningful and inclusive exchange of ideas. Just as a thoughtful host might accommodate different preferences and needs, educators creating an environment that supports diverse modes of communication empowers everyone to partake in the linguistic feast.

Like acquiring a foreign language requires learning its rules and vocabulary for comprehension, educating students with disabilities and living with disabilities both involve understanding that each person has distinct challenges. In similar ways to how unfamiliar sounds and structures in a new language affect a learner, my disabilities impacted how I was perceiving and interacting with the world as a child and a young adult, which definitely impacted my behavior.

Based on just the stories that I've shared in this book, it might seem easy to blame teachers for the many things that happened to me and my children. However, in a scenario where a teacher has several students with diverse challenges similar to mine, but lacks specific training in dealing with children with disabilities, the teacher might be overwhelmed and unsure about the best approach to take. The teacher might observe behaviors and struggles in their students that seem perplexing or challenging to address effectively.

Without training, the teacher might unintentionally misinterpret some behaviors as intentional or disruptive, rather than recognizing them as manifestations of underlying emotional, sensory or cognitive challenges. My difficulties with staying focused, following multi-step instructions, or responding to noise, for instance, could be misconstrued as a lack of attention or defiance. Similarly, my need for routines and aversion to change might be seen as resistance to adapting to the classroom environment.

In a situation where a teacher is ill-equipped, the teacher might apply traditional disciplinary measures or attempt to force conformity, leading to frustration for both the students and the teacher. A lack of understanding about sensory sensitivities could lead to unintentional sensory overload in the classroom, contributing to discomfort and heightened stress for students like me.

Due to the absence of disability training, teachers can struggle to differentiate between academic challenges and potential learning disabilities, which results in uneven support and missed opportunities for targeted interventions. Moreover, the teacher might overlook potential strengths and talents that students with disabilities possess. Obviously and unfortunately, I saw all of this as a special education teacher.

The same lack of training can also lead to caregivers and teachers stigmatizing children, which impacts the adults' ability to address the student's real challenges. This is what happened with the first- and second-grade teachers who stigmatized my student Nick and failed to recognize his growth. It's also what happened with the special education teacher who evaluated my oldest son; that teacher seemed to carry a prejudice when it came to my son's disability, largely influenced by her daughter's experience. Her belief that my son's difficulties were the same as her daughter's may have fueled her resistance to providing the necessary support.

Moreover, her accusation that I had influenced my son to think he was dyslexic—leading him to act as if he had the condition—pointed to her belief (and the belief of many) that learning disabilities are malleable and influenced by external factors. This viewpoint disregards the medical and psychological evaluations that confirmed my son's challenges, and it manifests a lack of empathy and understanding. It hindered the appropriate support and resources he needed to thrive in his educational journey. This situation caused trauma to our family, and it was a significant marker in our lives.

When that teacher and our family encountered each other in that situation, tensions were high, which hindered our ability to provide genuine mutual support.

I will never know for certain whether she had positive intentions or not, and I approached the situation carrying the weight of my own past experiences—ones marked by stigma and exclusion from my early educational years. These experiences were supplemented by the additional challenges I had faced as a parent. The compounding impact of poor care for students with disabilities is clear.

During our interactions, the teacher revealed that her own daughter had a disability. She communicated that despite their efforts, the outcomes remained unchanged. Therefore, she advised us to accept that our efforts might not significantly alter the trajectory of my son. Looking back, I believe this particular statement struck a chord within me. It marked the moment when I made judgments about her parenting abilities and questioned the value of her guidance. Which was also unfair because we were both doing our best to take care of our children and to support parents in our own way.

The teacher herself did not have a disability, and she made that point unmistakably clear. Consequently, I assumed that she had categorized her daughter based on an inability or unwillingness to disregard societal stigmas. However, I was unaware of her personal history, especially her experiences with her daughter. It took me a considerable amount of time to gain insight into how those experiences might have caused her to be affected by trauma. Adults frequently conceal their trauma beneath various facades, and educators often mask it by emphasizing research and a professional demeanor.

One significant challenge I didn't fully grasp when embarking on this journey was the profound impact of adversity on discovering my potential. While I had a personal understanding of both the concepts of adversity and potential, their implications were less clear.

Throughout my life, I have often been told that difficulties and setbacks were inevitable and that I should learn to cope with disappointment. Strife and adversity were bedfellows to disabilities, as I understood it, and they would result in intense conflict for me for the rest of my life. Instances of this very conflict marked my childhood.

But adversity denotes both enduring and severe misfortune, and the notion of misfortune or bad luck never sat well with me, especially when I try to apply it to my children's and my disabilities. The concept of bad luck felt like another layer of stigma applied to us. An essential step in confronting our situation was questioning whether my children were persistently embroiled in strife due to their disabilities and whether they should carry the notion that being disabled was equivalent to bad luck. Believing either of these ideas would essentially mean surrendering before even trying.

My disgust with the word "surrender" compelled me to seek ways to challenge the limitations society placed on me and my kids—limits they might never overcome, according to societal expectations. It wasn't about me imposing an arbitrary standard, it was about presenting an alternative perspective. Parenting is undoubtedly a demanding endeavor, and it becomes even more daunting when low expectations of your children are part of the equation.

Before kids, when it was just me, all I needed was to find shelter and eat. I wanted to be able to work in a sustainable job, and it didn't matter to me what that job was. I had no aspirations beyond survival. But when I had children, something lit inside of me. My focus became apparent, and I knew I needed to change—no one had to tell me. After spending years pushing to learn and acquire skills, I didn't want my kids to experience that life.

One might guess that I had a hero complex, but that wasn't it. I knew that they would have choices in their lives. I knew that their choices could lead them to hardship or success. But if I offered them up to a system that would give them the exact low expectations that I was provided, they would ultimately end up stuck, and that would be my fault for not stepping in when I could.

Teaching and learning are so important to me because I was denied quality education for so long due to the barrier of low expectations. The refusal to give someone information to help them grow is about power and control. Now, if someone does not want to hear the truth and refuses to use tools that could help them, that is their choice. I respect that choice and lean away. But if someone is asking to learn and if I have information to help them, I lean in—my body can't help it—it's just who I am.

But leaning toward someone can lead to immense possibilities. A coworker and I call it "rabbit holing"—digging in and discovering and learning and pursuing, even when there will always be more questions and your entire body is fatigued. I come alive in this space, which can be difficult for others; it's a space where I can give learners access to information and agency and let them choose where to take it. It took me some time to learn this teacherly gift in myself—and I didn't fully grasp it when I initially began teaching my children.

Let's face it: being a parent is complicated. Everyone on the planet has some "thoughtful" advice based on some lived or perceived experience on how to do it better. Most of that advice comes with little understanding of what it takes for another to implement those strategies in their life. I want to give you tools that you can apply and knowledge that you are not alone.

We often look at our resources and presume that we need to have what it takes to tackle the challenges we face. That is absolutely false. The most essential tools you need to get started are this book, writing utensils, and some paper. This is precisely where I got started. If you have additional supplies, WONDERFUL! That is not a requirement.

Think about it like this: Imagine two artists; one has access to nothing more than the dirt in front of them, and the other has access to the most expensive art supplies available. Who will create the best masterpiece? The answer is that their ability to produce art does not depend on the tools they have; it depends on their willingness to use what they have to create. Both could create a masterpiece or not.

Working with a child who is behind, for whatever reason, requires you to have a willingness to use the tools around you to be creative. I shared my story here to help you to understand that we did not have much. We did not begin with a considerable level of knowledge about the process. We practiced skills and developed strategies over time. Your journey might take you down a different path, which is fine.

When I initially began working with my daughter, she fought with me. Somehow, eventually, we found our stride. When I started working with my oldest son, we went back and forth between "today is a great day" to "today is an interesting event for both of us." With him, I needed more community support. I still worked with him, but I did not do that work alone. With my youngest son, even though we worked together, his siblings were his greatest teachers. He and I have been discovering how we live as individuals with autism, and while I am very impressed with his natural intelligence and kindness, his siblings also used what I did with them to teach him. I'm still uncovering how to support him as a parent, but knowing that information helps me. The fact is that communication—between parents and children and between any individuals in a relationship—is a never-ending process. It requires work from two parties, and I will always have space to grow and learn with every human I am in contact with.

Our family needed to learn a variety of skills and we needed a wide range of tools. Because of allergies, we spent limited amounts of time outside. We used a lot of paper—I should have invested in a paper supply company! My favorite tools are pencil and paper, but those are not the only tools. Start with what you have and add to your toolbox over time. Once you understand where you need to start, the next most important resource you have at your disposal is the content that you have to teach.

I was learning alongside my children; to pretend otherwise is ridiculous. My children needed to see me struggle and they needed to watch me grow from the experience. It is important for all of us to understand that someone might struggle with relaying information in a variety of ways, and that should not prohibit them from developing and learning job readiness skills. I've had people tell me that I was not qualified to teach my children because I could teach them coping skills, but my options for giving them strong content were limited. Thus, my "coping skill" methodology was the tool we needed to use. This consumed my time and that is the next most important item that parents/teachers/caregivers need to consider.

Finding resources in your community can be difficult. Especially when most services appear to be cost-driven. I started initially by reaching out to friends and looking at ways we could help one another. The babysitter that my youngest son loved would attend zoo trips with us from time to time. That helped my youngest son develop social skills. Some teachers offered after-school classes for students, and I would attend with my children and learn some strategies to help teach them. You will find similar resources, or you will find some of your own. When teachers and caregivers understand the differences in how people with disabilities learn, they help all students.

If teachers knew what I was facing as a student, they could have supported me earlier in my academic life. The only way for them to know now is if I speak out because many of us cannot articulate our struggles to others. There are several examples of that in this book. My young second-grade friend from Chapter 8 was being asked to read before he could work with the symbols of writing. When we had him speak (which was where his trauma had cut him off) and then practice the symbols of writing, he was able to produce the shape of letters, and eventually, he was able to read the words. His confidence and skill building were developed and confirmed when he could teach.

I wish his teacher would have attended his final reading session with me. She would have seen him read and explain a second-grade text to his younger peers and his sixth-grade mentor. The purpose of sharing his story in this text is not to blame the teachers. Teachers have their own trauma and deserve the right to feel hurt by it. Being grown up does not make dealing with trauma easy. His teacher was, in many ways, overwhelmed. She had several high-needs students in her class, and she needed the right skills to deal with them all. We must acknowledge that both students and teachers need better support.

How this teacher felt must have been similar to how my mother felt when I was younger. Also, the teachers I encountered as a child were in an even more challenging position because they didn't have as much knowledge as we currently do about disabilities or differences. I could not have articulated any of my experiences then, and so my only entry into the space of understanding disability was through the research of experts, who were working hard (in my opinion) to figure out solutions. Still, I have been privileged to live a tremendously blessed life.

I have benefited from every struggle and triumph. It took me many years to forgive and thank my mom. She and I must have been a lot alike, given how much we struggled so much with one another. At times, I thought I hated her; other times, I was sure she hated me. A week before she passed away, I heard from her mouth that my assumptions were inaccurate. I'm forever thankful for that final conversation. I'm also very thankful for the moments we spent together, though they were limited. My mother left me the gift of tenacity. She may not have understood what her actions did to me, but I learned survival skills due to the situations she put me in. She also taught me that beauty can be found in anything. She was a fantastic artist. She could take something absolutely junk and turn it into something beautiful. The impact of her artistry on me came to life the moment that I began to paint and discovered I could retain information through this creative act.

In 2017, when my mother apologized to me, she left me with hope. Though it doesn't justify the experience I had with her as a child, she gave me skills I needed to survive. My time with my mom also helped me to realize that I have a purpose in life – to see into a space that few people get a glimpse into.

My father, whose name was Joseph, and I took a different path. I had been told my entire life that my father had abandoned us. By age fifteen, I was a bitterly rocked soul. At that time, I was using partial sentences to express my thoughts, partly because I was struggling to understand sentence structure—I could not, at that age, tell you the difference between a noun, verb, adjective, and adverb. My father visited with some of his brothers, and I threw a sadly constructed poem, made of sections of fragmented sentences, in his face and yelled at him for leaving me. Instead of screaming, my father dropped to his knees and wept—apologizing to me and begging for forgiveness. No adult had ever apologized to me in my life. It shook me fiercely and to my core. He then asked me to take a walk.

After that day, we walked miles and miles together, sharing all the conversations we had missed for fifteen years. During our walks, he taught me about forgiveness and kindness. He told me my anger was killing me, and I was in control of that death. He said I had to forgive my mother and grandmother for keeping me from him. It didn't make sense that he was pleading with me on their behalf. Yet, there he was, demanding that I let it go, ease the tension from my shoulders, and breathe as we walked.

My father never yelled at me. No matter what I did. From what I can remember, he never yelled at anyone; he always forgave people. When I learned he was terminally ill in 2002, I visited him in a home for retired and disabled veterans. To my surprise, that day he yelled at me. There I was, thirty years old, and he yelled that I was not doing enough with my life. At the time, I had five kids, a full-time job, and I was in school full-time learning to communicate. I was confused, but he had a letter-size manila envelope on his lap. Dad reached into the envelope and pulled out the poem I had thrown at him as an angry teenager. He'd held on to it for over fifteen years. I hadn't even realized that he even picked it up off the floor. He told me he wanted to be proud of me and that I had more inside of me than I was showing. He told me to do something with that poem and my life. He also commanded me to start telling people when they fed into my life, even if it was just through a small gesture. He ended that conversation by telling me to accept that his life was ending. Four months later, he was gone.

My dad, Joseph, and I.

What I learned from that day was that my life was not meaningless. My journey through my own disabilities helped me to be the mother of children with disabilities. If I had not experienced what it was like to be marginalized or come to understand what the educational system could and couldn't provide, I might have left my children's progress to others and missed the miracles. Had I not worked with my own children, I would not have realized that I had learned and mastered the skill of teaching. I would not have been a strong special education teacher, corporate trainer, or program designer. It was all for a reason.

About
Kharis Publishing:

Kharis Publishing, an imprint of Kharis Media LLC, is a leading Christian and inspirational book publisher based in Aurora, Chicago metropolitan area, Illinois. Kharis' dual mission is to give voice to under-represented writers (including women and first-time authors) and equip orphans in developing countries with literacy tools. That is why, for each book sold, the publisher channels some of the proceeds into providing books and computers for orphanages in developing countries so that these kids may learn to read, dream, and grow. For a limited time, Kharis Publishing is accepting unsolicited queries for nonfiction (Christian, self-help, memoirs, business, health and wellness) from qualified leaders, professionals, pastors, and ministers. Learn more at: https://kharispublishing.com/

www.ingramcontent.com/pod-product-compliance
Lightning Source LLC
Chambersburg PA
CBHW062108080426
42734CB00012B/2800